The Naked Millionaire

The Naked Millionaire

A women's guide to building a healthy relationship with money

Maxine Hyndman

INSOMNIAC PRESS

Library and Archives Canada Cataloguing in Publication

Hyndman, Maxine C., 1965-
  The naked millionaire : a women's guide to building a healthy
relationship with money / Maxine C. Hyndman.

Includes index.
ISBN 1-894663-87-X

  1. Finance, Personal. I. Title.

HG179.H95 2005   332.024   C2005-900246-8

The publisher gratefully acknowledges the support of the
Canada Council, the Ontario Arts Council and the Department of
Canadian Heritage through the Book Publishing Industry
Development Program.

Printed and bound in Canada

Insomniac Press
192 Spadina Avenue, Suite 403
Toronto, Ontario, Canada, M5T 2C2
www.insomniacpress.com

Dedication

First and foremost I thank my family for always being there for me in the good and not so good money times of my life; for their support whenever I was at my lowest, and when I was afraid to break through my past into greater things.

I thank my daughter for her wisdom and flexibility while I was finding my Greater Purpose, there is no price for what you give me everyday.

I thank D.B. for throughout the writing of this book. You were the example of financial grounding I looked to for inspiration. I'll bet you didn't know that, did you?

Finally, This book is dedicated to anyone feeling as if their financial burden is insurmountable and that their money problems are hopeless; to anyone drowning in debt with barely enough energy to get out of bed in the morning.

I will show you that it is possible, that you can obtain financial health. It is not money that gives your life meaning, it is what you do with that life that does.

May you be a constant vessel for abundance, in all its various forms and dimensions.

Contents

Introduction

Approximately 4 million people declared bankruptcy in America between 1998 and 2000, and in North America 2.8 million people filed for bankruptcy between the years 2000 and 2001. Astonishingly, within America 1.4 million bankruptcies were filed in 1998—this was a year of record-high economic prosperity. The nation's outstanding credit-card debt had hit a high of $635 billion in 2000, while the savings rate is at a negative. Five years ago I was part of this statistic.

Household debt is a disease that plagues individuals and families throughout North America. There are very few people who know how to deal with money effectively, much less build financial-wellness from cinder and ash. We're all familiar with the adages "It takes money to make money... Another day another dollar..." Well, beliefs like these are at the heart of the financial burdens that many North American people struggle with today. Bankruptcy is one of these burdens. While they are recovering from bankruptcy or financial crisis, many bright people want to make a lot of money, improve their credit rating, or pay off old debts; but few who waded through the mire of financial crisis or bankruptcy actually seek financial-wellness, or *whealth*, as I call it. How many people actually try to cultivate a state of financial-wholeness, or desire to lift themselves from the pit of always needing or wanting more? How many people actually reconfigure their perspective of what financial-wellness is by first mastering their money strategies? Far too often, the desire for more money is all pervading, spreading like a mirage in our minds; an illusion of happiness that will not quell our inner yearnings.

We experience a financial divide because something within us rejects spiritual abundance, or whealth. This book will allow you to accept more, clear away unproductive money patterns, and soon you will start building your foundation for whealth. Everyday, you will build on the exercises and tools included in this guide, bringing along your own life experience and expertise. This approach will provide you with your own *living tools*. This book is not about the technical aspects of financial recovery: you won't find detailed approaches to RRSPs, 401Ks, or insurance products. What you *will* find are practical applications for building financial-health from the inside-out. You will learn how to change your perceptions of money, and your new outlook will eventually send money your way. You'll learn how to clean the slate and start fresh; how to create a financial structure that will be strong enough to survive any circumstance. You'll learn to stay on track, establish financial trust with yourself, and you will create buying habits that support your new direction. This book seeks to put money into its proper place because, in reality, money is only a small facet of a much greater whole. There are many books which deal with financial education, but it's important to understand that money problems have very little, if anything, to do with money and everything to do with the relationship we share with it.

A teacher of mine once told my class that he and his wife sat down one night before to work out their will. The process, he said, was so unsettling that it drove his wife to tears. This story intrigued me because I wondered why working out a will might bring someone to the point of tears. In performing my research for this book, I began to understand that the questions we are forced to answer when preparing a will are far more soul searching than the process of requesting a loan. These questions necessitate that we reach deep into ourselves and they force us to evaluate our current environment for answers. Facing our realities can be both frightening and overwhelming. Difficult questions arise, such as "How do I administer funds to my children if they are not very good at managing money? What should I do if the child's appointed guardian isn't good at handling money? Am I even competent during the writing of the will? Am I considered healthy during the writing of the will?" The list could go on and on. It seemed to me that controlling whealth after death, whether we have heirs or not, is more important than mastering the ability to create and manage whealth during our lifetimes. Odd.

Before a university student receives their first credit card does anyone ask about their financial-wellness? Is anyone concerned about their level of financial literacy or competence? Are any consultations required to identify their values and define a budget around these values? Similarly, are any deep questions asked during, or at the discharge of bankruptcy? In every instance, the answer is "no." Instead, I was required to attend two meetings in the nine months after my bankruptcy where I was asked elementary questions, a few of which included "Did you apply for credit in the last four weeks? Are you currently employed? What's your job title now and how much are you currently making? Did you have a salary increase in the last three months? Do you understand what led to your bankruptcy?" (Was that a trick question?)

Later, when I paid $900 to a credit restoration firm so I could rebuild my credit, they did not ask me any pertinent questions about my overall financial-wellness. Their only duty was to make me creditworthy as soon as possible. And how was this miracle going to happen, I wondered? By securing a credit card, making small purchases and paying them off, of course. Now I could get back into the game

Greater Purpose

Your Greater Purpose is what you were meant to bring here since you first arrived. It is your unique contribution to making your world a better place. It's what makes you light up when you talk about it or you're engaged in it. Engaging in your greater purpose fills you up on all levels and almost never leaves you feeling drained. It is your direct connection to the divine.

and start the ball rolling without more than a hiccup—but this wasn't what I wanted. I wanted to earn the kind of whealth that would last and allow me to weather any storm. I wanted someone to show me how this could be done, but no one was interested in my inability to sustain financial-health. No one, that was, but me. I knew that if I didn't do something about my financial situation, I would slowly decline, and I wasn't sure where this decline would take me.

In our society the anticipation of death forces us to think about our money and how we would like it to be managed after we're gone. While writing this book I kept in mind that financial crisis, especially bankruptcy, is a type of death, and that the journey to financial-wellness entails the same future focus that crafting a will includes. We must start thinking and acting beyond the next payday, the next two weeks, two months, or the next two years. We've got to think *big* when it comes to our money. I'm not saying "imagine yourself with one million dollars."

The Big Picture I'm speaking of has to do with your Greater Purpose, your Values, your Trust, and finally the creation of an Ethical Will, or the *context* of money.

The Naked Millionaire is a resource, the starting point towards financial-wholeness and health. It involves all aspects of yourself, not just the part that earns a living, or the part of you that worries about money. These pages urge you to tap into every aspect of yourself, aligning all areas of your being. In my mind, whealth is first and foremost about self-literacy and self-healing. Throughout most of my life I have felt whealthy inside, but I've always struggled to align my inner world with my outer reality. I had to stop deluding myself with the "money lies" that allowed me to live beyond my means, and I had to get naked and face my financial reality. True whealth can only be acquired, and sustained, if we are realistic about what we can afford in the moment.

I've come a long way, realizing that it *isn't* about money as much as it really *is*. This might sound paradoxical but

Ethical Will

Ethical will, similar to a will, but you are passing on a wealth of values, wisdom, and insight to the next generation—not your possessions. As time passes and certain fundamental pillars of what it means to be a human being erode— pillars like intuition, trust, and integrity—your stories of how these hold together your family, will light the way for generations to come.

it's the truth. Whealth isn't about the dollars—it's about the *sense*. The real prize is finding the lifestyle that fits you best; one that will make *sense* as well as cents.

When you look at pictures of yourself from high school, you might shake your head at the ridiculous outfits you once thought were so cool. "What was I thinking?" you ask. You know better now. Now you choose clothing that reflects who you are because you aren't so obsessed with fitting in with a crowd. When we follow our instincts and act as individuals, we come closer to achieving a lifestyle that suits our individual needs. I have found that my writing is an integral part of who I am. I'm no longer willing to compromise my values for work that pays "big bucks." I only take work that is rewarding, both spiritually and financially.

I became really interested in money and my relationship with it when I filed for bankruptcy. I now believe that financial literacy is as important to us as a university education is to a student who aspires to become a lawyer or a doctor. It is my wish and my intent to inspire in you a mastery over money, and it is my hope that you will pass this wisdom along to your future generations.

Chapter One
Fear and Loathing in My Wallet

I've come to understand a basic life equation that I call the Effort Equation. It is based on the following premise: (focused effort + innovation = increase). Let's look at this closely for a moment. Why is understanding how we struggle important to our financial health? It's important because if we are experiencing any form of money pain, we are involved in a struggle. Often, we believe that the path of struggle is a noble path because at least we are trying. But even if we are advancing, no matter how far, struggle is always futile and it is a waste of precious energy. Bill Gates did not become a billionaire by toiling in a manufacturing plant from nine-to-five. Gates used his creative powers to invent software for the masses. In the years to come, the people who earn the most will be those who focus their energy and efforts on innovation. Whole economies can crumble when the equation (focused effort + innovation = greater increase) is ignored. Take, for example, Argentina. In 2001 Argentina went through an enormous economic crisis. This economic crisis was felt mainly by the middle class, and many businesses and households had been forced into bankruptcy. An article in the Canadian edition of *Time* stated that "….until Argentines build an economy based less on beef than on brainpower, their century-old decline will never end." So what does Argentina and the Effort Equation have to do with whealth? Everything! For too long Argentina focused on beef, not innovation, and now their economy is crumbling. Argentina's focus had been too narrow, and perhaps it is time that they start searching for whealth elsewhere. If we don't focus on the right things, as times change, our own personal economies will also crumble.

Effort is struggle, not work. And that is what most people are used to—struggle. We struggle to make ends meet, struggle to keep afloat through downsizing, or when the government decides to raise taxes or introduce a new tax. When I first started this business, I still believed that struggle was unavoidable. I had witnessed a lot of hardship during childhood, so I was accustomed to struggle, and I accepted it too readily. For almost seven years I felt like I was banging my head against the wall because I had been convinced that "the first three years in business are always the toughest." I thought, just grin and bare it, Maxine, this is normal. I generated very small sales, depleted my energies, had bouts of serious depression, and I completely drained my funds. I was caught in a cycle of *struggle*, and I was unaware that nothing was *working*. Later, when I started as a freelance copywriter, my first client was essentially served to me on a platter. My computer technician came to fix my computer, and he ended up fixing my computer for free. To show my gratitude I offered to help him write any content he might need in the future. He said that one of his clients needed this type of help, and I ended up designing the site's creative and content flow. My first client came to me by very little effort. I landed this first job because I communicated my services to someone who was receptive. This was difficult for me, but having faith in my writing abilities paid off. I challenge you to retire your belief in struggle. Put it to rest, forever. Do this and you'll notice a change in your life—that's a promise.

After a financial crisis, it is a slow, sometimes painful road to recovery, so don't let anyone fool you into thinking it isn't. If it isn't, you're not really healing. Six months after being discharged from bankruptcy I was still grappling with the effects of my decision. Why wasn't I feeling better? What I learned was that even though I was discharged from the courts, I hadn't yet cured the *dis-ease* that had originally caused my crisis.

For many people, it's much easier to talk about sex or abortion than it is about money. If we can't talk about an issue, we can't heal it. And since we all have a story, I'm going to start with my own.

I don't know when my relationship with money became so tortured, but it did. One day, I was a child accumulating savings in my account, and the next you know I was a teenager who borrowed money from friends for lunch. Eventually, I found myself as a single, divorced mother borrowing money from the government. My money problems crept up on me, unannounced and uninvited. I assumed it was due to just one thing, one incident, but it wasn't. Really, I was afraid to uncover the true source of my bankruptcy. I believed that I was building a business, and when it went bust, I decided to build another one on top of the rubble. I was unable to face the hurt that rested just beneath the surface: the flawed perception about money I carried with me was "Nothing will ever come easy to you. You've got to work three times as hard as others to prove you worth." It's messed up, I know, but there it was. My unhealthy relationship with money sprang from many of the destructive feelings I had about who I was as a person. It also dictated how I conducted my friendships and business, but mostly these feelings of failure and doubt further infected my sense of self, my well-being. I don't know when I stopped loving myself enough, stopped having confidence in who I was and what I could accomplish. But I did, and eventually I was bankrupt within.

I began experiencing a deficit: the amount by which something is less than what is required or expected. The way my life communicated this to me was financially. I had gone though a divorce—a very amicable one, but I didn't realize that it had drained me, and so instead of rejuvenating my resources by taking time for me, I propelled myself into a fury of unfulfilling work, ignoring the pain and shame I still harboured inside. I was hurting. I had left someone I cared about, taking my daughter away from her father, and leaving a country I had called home for eight years. I didn't love myself enough to honour the anguish I was going through. I didn't know that my resolve had its limits. Very slowly, I learned that I had become bankrupt because I was not listening. I was unconscious of my own needs, and this is how bankruptcy begins for all of us.

As I began to awaken I wondered why, with the proliferation of so many self-help books, are people still going broke, declaring bankruptcy, and juggling such heavy financial burdens? I was amazed at how many books on investing there were: smart investing, simple investing, beating the analysts, beating Wall Street. I realized that many people don't have a healthy relationship with money.

Financial dis-ease begins in the heart, infects the mind, and finally it presents itself as a physical reality, actualizing itself in bankruptcy, foreclosure, or crisis. When you have nothing else to give yourself or others, when you can no longer "pay" yourself then you are bankrupt. What I mean by pay is a currency of love, trust, time, understanding, appreciation, and forgiveness. When you pay yourself in this currency you are actually filling up your "credit" account, an account you can draw from in times of need. Overwork, the wrong work, no leisure time, unwise life choices—all of these drain our accounts. In short, we have to "pay" ourselves on a regular basis.

While writing this book I discussed the title with my daughter. She asked me why I used the word "Naked." I had only thought about my reasons briefly, but now I had to explain them, and the reasons became clear as I told her: "by 'Naked' I mean that we have nowhere to hide and that we must face the truth and stop lying about our financial

states, and our relations with money." I also wanted anyone reading this to be honest and unashamed about their
relationship with money, and through reading this, to
heighten their level of whealth consciousness.

I have lied to myself about money. I have told myself
that it doesn't matter; that it only makes good people do
bad things or it changes who they are, and that I was actually happier without it. I told myself all kinds of things
because I couldn't admit that I had no control over money
and that this fact was ruining my life. When we look into
why we become bankrupt, we see that we have limited
belief systems, along which our thoughts flow—our
thoughts, like grooves on a record will continue along this
path and our reality will be based on these thoughts. These

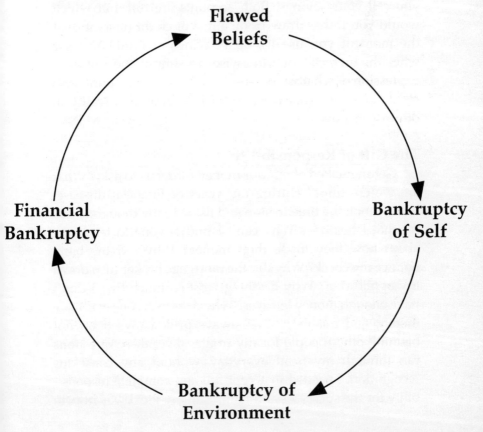

systems are limited. What we have to do is rewire, and create new paths, and we cannot succumb to old habits or learned behaviours. Whealth is a natural state of being, one that we are all entitled to, but we must consciously choose whealth as a way of life.

Let's take a look at whealth in terms of values. What do you value? If something (possession, person, pet, belief) was taken away, what could you not live without? Write these on a piece of paper. What you're making is a list of what you value. Get the picture? If after looking at your list you realize it consists of things like the approval of others, attention, possessions, then you are increasing your line of credit, or debt. Or, do you value fresh air, being with friends, laughter, balance, and harmony. Then this is what you call your savings. Both accounts are full, but which would you rather draw from: a line of credit (instant debt the moment you use it), or a savings account? You see whealth, financial or otherwise, is simply the outward expression of what we possess in our internal accounts. We must *possess* internal whealth for it to become a reality in our external lives.

The Gift of Responsibility

Getting naked about our money forces us to ask, "What are we creating?" During my years of financial dis-ease, when I took the time to stop and listen to my thoughts, this is what I heard—"Why can't I find anyone to teach me about how they made their money? Why did the bank bounce my check? Why did the mortgage broker turn down my application? Why do things cost so much that I don't have enough money leftover? Why does everyone else have money, and not me?" I've always prided myself on not blaming other people for my troubles, yet these questions ran through my head everyday, without any conscious recognition. I needed to accept full and complete responsibility for the successes and failures in my life. I was in pain because I wasn't claiming all of it, I wasn't owning my creation, and I needed to do this before I could have whealth.

People were hounding me because I was afraid; they were being unkind and disrespectful because I didn't have any respect or kindness for myself; the mortgage broker turned me down because I turned myself down; I couldn't find someone to show me how to build a successful business because there was still a place within me that rejected success. People don't reject whealth you say! Oh, yes they do, and the fact that so many millions are declaring bankruptcy and not saving just shows us how many people do reject whealth. A foundation of erroneous beliefs held together by a strong sense of unworthiness is the biggest cause of this dis-ease.

Remember that the definition of wealth is the possession of a *large* amount of money, property, or any *other valuable thing*—a large amount. Not just enough. If we were put on earth with just enough trees, many of us would not be here today because we would have run out by now.

Since human beings are creators, striving to make our lives better through creating, taking responsibility for *all* of our creations, apparently good or bad, is the first step in whealth consciousness. *Responsibility is simply being in a position where you will be liable to be called to account as the primary cause, motive, or agent*—nothing more, nothing less. Financial healing involves making continuous adjustments. Taking responsibility for your financial health is an important adjustment in your journey towards whealth.

An adjustment is a shift in consciousness, an alteration, or correction that you make, just as chiropractic realignments to the spine might be necessary at times. Tiny financial adjustments over time, one by one, make all the difference in the world, and they don't have to be painful; adjustments such as financial education, saving, realizing your Greater Purpose, or volunteering will help. Financial responsibility is also your state of *acceptance*, it is also the state of being awake rather than being asleep or uncon-scious. Going through bankruptcy awoke me from finan-cial slumber. A part of me was asleep and I was unable to respond to external economic stresses. I was irresponsible.

What tiny adjustments can you make? How can you better your relationship with money? What are you willing to accept? Are you willing to accept an adjustment in your perception of what is enough? Are you willing to accept an increase of money in your life? These are all very important questions that you must ask yourself.

I made many adjustments during and after bankruptcy, and many of these changes were subtle. I kept a log of my monthly bills, I wrote out a "want list," and then a list of other debts that needed to be paid. I went and found a job and I invited more into every area of my life—even if some-one wanted to take me out to lunch and I could pay, I allowed them to treat me and said, "Yes! Thank you!" I accepted gifts and praise. Accepting these pleasures was once very difficult for me, but as time went on, I began talk-ing to myself more kindly and with more patience. It is strange, many of us would never dream of being as biting and heartless with a stranger on the street as we are with ourselves. I began visualizing myself with more and I recit-ed this prayer: "Thank you God for all of the blessings that I have and for all of the blessings that I am receiving." I for-gave myself for going bankrupt and I gave thanks for the experience of bankruptcy; without it I would have never rediscovered writing and my desire to help others.

Emerging from bankruptcy felt like a new beginning for me. It felt like a second chance to prove to myself that I am worthy of financial health. In spite of everything, my outward reality was showing me I possessed whealth; and that all I had to do now was put it into action. Bankruptcy revealed my erroneous money beliefs. It bit and tore away my fears of ridicule and ostracism—fears that I believe many of us have. I realized that something can be gained in any experience, and that even the ugliest times are always a gift. When I rose from my financial slumber I read everything I could on personal finance, balance sheets, budgets, taxes, real estate, stock investing, and building businesses. I wanted to become acquainted with my money, and any debts I still had, and I wanted to know it like the back of my hand. As I did this I felt the rubber band that had been stretched so taut, begin to ease. I felt I could control it. Every time I began to worry over this or that money problem, I would talk to myself and fill my thoughts with words and visions of what I wanted in my life. The anxiety began to fade. As though I were Sleeping Beauty, I saw economic hardship as a kiss that awoke within me a respect and awareness of whealth. I was finally gaining the strength to respond to the financial demands in my life. I awoke to a new groove.

Chapter Two

A New Groove

In the previous chapter we looked at owning all of our creations, good or bad, including our money messes. Now we need to look at improving the source of our money creations—our belief systems.

Before cassette tapes and CDs, we listened to LPs (long-playing records). These long-playing records had grooves which held the actual music. Even if you played that record a thousand times, it would always play the same music in the same sequence or pattern. This is because they came pre-etched. Now we have CD writers, as well as the Internet and personal computers that give us the freedom to choose the songs we want to write or imprint on a different CD. Even better, if you are bored of it, or if you don't like the way you mixed the music, you can change the order of the songs, add new ones, or delete the old ones by rewriting over the old songs. I use this example because this analogy illustrates how we allow our minds to be programmed by our past failures. Our belief systems are like grooves, and we often become caught in these grooves, many of which are injurious to our well-being. When we accept more and try different ways of doing things, we can erase and rewrite many of the questionable beliefs we've held for a long, long time. So let's say it's been a month since you've established new beliefs, but now these beliefs are beginning to lose their power. This happens because we are constantly changing and our energies are constantly being drained and recharged. Not to worry. You can simply rewrite those beliefs again until they feel right and soon the music of your life will flow smoothly. For example, one of my old beliefs used to be, "I'll never have enough money for everything I want. I am unhappy." This was a negative groove that played non-stop in the back of my head, similar to that annoying elevator music that stays in your head long after you have left the store. I rewired this belief to, "I am happy. I am being richly rewarded for doing what I love." Eventually, the truth, when I could accept it, became clear and simple: "I am a happy person." My world began to reflect this belief. If you stop to evaluate your eternal music, you'll be surprised at what you hear. Stop and listen to it as many times as you need. Letting go of belief systems that no longer work for you is one of the toughest challenges you'll face on your journey to recovery.

What a lot of people don't understand is that we've got to give something up for things to change. That's right. And here's the tough part—giving up might not always be about money or material objects. Often, when we make inner changes we must let go of outdated, harmful beliefs. Sounds easy, right? Actually it's one of the hardest things to do. This is why millions of people find it easier to declare bankruptcy, or cut up their credit cards, rather than change beliefs that no longer work for them. For example, you have to stop thinking in a certain way, saying or thinking certain words, or accepting certain negative phrases as truth from close friends and family. You might have to stop believing you are worthless, that there is no hope, or that you can't trust yourself to go out with $1,000 in your wallet for fear you'll spend it. You'll have to stop believing that there are groups of people who want to see you oppressed, or that you have nothing of value to offer the world. When you embark on this new groove, you'll be continuously reminding yourself that you *are* valuable, that people *do* want to just give you things, and that things can come to you easily and effortlessly. Even if you don't know who

they are, people do love you, and they want to see you succeed.

Let's look at why we might cling to hurtful beliefs. I
believe that one of the biggest reasons is guilt. Often, for no
reason at all, we feel like we've done something wrong and
that we should be punished. We might fear success because
we are afraid of leaving our friends and family behind,
especially if they too struggle for financial-wellness. There
is nothing wrong with being whealthy, prospering, and
maintaining financial health. Would you deny yourself, or
anyone else, physical health? Do you believe there would
not be enough health for everyone else if you enjoyed more
than enough good health? Then why do we think about
financial health in such negative terms? It is true, you
might have to give up old friends and family that no longer
support your new groove, but this doesn't mean they
might not become curious about your new music and want
to listen, or even start dancing to a similar tune. They might
even become curious about what *their* new groove could
sound like.

Rewiring Beliefs

Do you know what your beliefs look like? Or what they
feel like? Or how they present themselves in your body?
Getting to know your beliefs is a very important part of
your financial healing. Some of the outdated beliefs many
of us still have about money are— "money doesn't grow on
trees; I've worked hard for my money; it's easier for a
camel to pass through the eye of a needle than for a rich
man to enter Heaven; filthy rich; money changes people;
money is the root of all evil; money can't buy you happiness / love; if it's not feast, it's famine..." On and on it
goes. What money misconceptions do you hold? List as
many as you can. Take an honest look at them. The two of
you need to get better acquainted. In doing so you are shining new light on notions that are ingrained in you, that

have been buried for a very long time. These beliefs have come to be your companions, no matter how hurtful they have been, or how much pain and distress they have caused in your life. To illustrate exactly what I mean, here is a reflection from my personal journal: "Today my mother and I were talking and she suggested that I am afraid of success because I have known failure, and failure is something I'm comfortable with. This hit home as truth. Like many people, I know failure intimately and so I try to cling to it as things begin to break for success in my life—it's a dingy with a hole, but still a dingy. I need to make peace with that part of my life and let it go because it is no longer serving a purpose in my life. It's familiar, cozy and it's come to be a close, personal friend of mine. But I no longer need this hardship; you are free to go now. I am ready to learn other things that you will never teach me. I've come to know walls and ceilings, with their cracks and leaks, all too well. This shell of poverty, or at the very best, this *not enough*, has haunted me long enough. I've told it—asked it—to leave because it was an intimate friend I had known all my life. It taught me the beliefs I now have and it helped me with the selection of friends it thought I was best suited for. It told me, or rather, established what I would earn and who I would most likely choose to marry. It even helped me fall into the arms of government support that I was entitled to receive because of my plight—you know, single mother, no job...

"But I've kept you around long enough," I continued writing, "Like a ratty, old blanket at the age of 35—nonsense! I know you've had the best intentions my old friend, you had my well-being at heart, but I must say goodbye. I must be bold and courageous enough to say goodbye. And ask that you never return. I have a new companion for the rest of my journey: I have invited abundance into my life to guide me and teach me things you cannot. From you, failure / poverty I have learned much; gratitude, continuity, grace under pressure, the value of true beauty, and so much more. You are free to go. I release you from your services. Success will take me onward now. Thank you." The bond we have with our perceptions of money is so emotional, so powerful that breaking it takes love, a gentle kindness and a vision, not force.

When I talk about the cultivation of a "new vision" for your life, I am talking about vision as being the offspring of visualization, and when we change our beliefs we need to incorporate the power of visualization because it helps us connect on an emotional level with a reality that has yet to be established. Our new beliefs are still nebulous, not yet strong enough to be held up to cold scrutiny. Visualizing your new beliefs will strengthen them. For example, I mentioned that my new belief was "I am happy. I am being richly rewarded for what I have done." I had to also accompany this with an emotional "charge" to kick-start the belief into action. I visualized myself smiling from ear to ear. I felt my chest become lighter and

Visualization

Visualization is the act of consciously believing a possible reality different from the one you are currently living. In visualizing this new reality the conscious stimulation of all the five senses are put into play— sight, smell, hearing, touch, and taste. Visualization is the active ingredient of our dreams.

.ny whole body tingled as I imagined myself sharing this book with large groups of women. My whole being became charged with a lightness, a joy. I *was* happy. The results of my visualization exercise were exactly the same as when I experienced happiness in my outer world. Saying and writing your beliefs is a good place to start, but when you begin to visualize your beliefs, you are building a new foundation, a structure that will be the framework for a whealthy you. Visualization is the act of consciously believing in a proposed reality that is different from the one you are currently living. Visualization makes our dreams come to life.

What have you learned from poverty consciousness? What blessings has it given you? Write them down. Then, visualize a way out of your old ruts and patterns. Where do you want to be? What can you achieve? Be grateful for what these beliefs have taught you then say goodbye. See them as if personified, walking away up a hill, through a pasture; then see yourself turn around and walk away. Until I saw poverty hanging around me like an old blanket, I didn't even know that I kept it close, or that I felt waves of anxiety anytime whealth drew near. We are the only ones who keep ourselves imprisoned by our fear of failure, and we are the only ones who can break these chains and take whealth by the hand. Get to know yourself better than you know anyone or anything else in the world—better than you know your husband, your children, or your job. Be kind to yourself, treat yourself with the greatest love and respect. Making the adjustment also means refilling the places you extract from. You've just said goodbye to an old friend and now you've got to replace it. We all know the lawn treatment Weed 'N Feed. This lawn spray *removes* the weeds and *feeds* the grass at the same time. We must adopt a similar process; by replacing old beliefs with new ones, we will establish a healthier, more positive sense of self. Some new beliefs that I've embraced are: I have more than enough money for all of my needs and wants; money is coming to me easily and effortlessly; I am whealthy; I choose happiness. I choose to believe in these ideals, in spite of my outward reality. I realized this outward reality was only a reflection of everything that I believed in the past. I am now in the present, and, to make a change, this is where you have to be too.

The Illusion

Why does it seem that the harder you try to fix your financial problems, the worse your money problems get? You've tried to implement the new beliefs, but the old ones just keep coming back to haunt you. Some days, progress seems impossible and you're almost ready to give up. This is the illusion. For those of you not familiar with naturopathy, it is a distinct system of healing—a philosophy, a science, an art, and a practice—which seeks to promote health by stimulating and supporting the body's inherent power to regain harmony and balance. Although the term naturopathy was first used at the turn of the 20th century, the philosophical basis and many of the methods of naturopathic medicine are ancient, some dating back to at least 400 B.C.E., when Hippocrates became famous for his treatment of disease in accordance with natural laws.

The principles of naturopathy are—

1. Only nature heals, provided it is given the opportunity to do so.
2. Let food be your medicine and let medicine be your food.
3. Disease is an expression of purification.
4. All disease is one.

Naturopathy believes that disease occurs when the vital life force must expend energy, removing any obstructions that block the normal functioning of organs and tissues. A healthy functioning of our financial lives is often obstructed by our beliefs. So when bankruptcy, or financial crisis is driven by unfounded misconceptions, when we change our groove and start believing in new, more empowering concepts, there will be disturbances—diseases—and perhaps even other financial crises. But, these disturbances are caused because our vital energy is removing those hindering mental obstructions. So the illusion that change causes more grief—more creditors call, your car breaks down and costs you a pile of money, your landlord raises the rent—is only part of a transition which will eventually lead to greater stability. Don't give up, it is just your life trying to heal itself. A part of your old self is still grappling with this new, improved self, but your wiser self will triumph and you will find peace.

Keep visualizing and reaffirming your new beliefs, and trust that you have the power to change the old patterns in your life. As you are working your way towards financial health, stay focused on what you want, where you want to be, and on the tiny, little successes you have each day. You might see your new thoughts reflected on the billboards you notice on the street, on license plates, or in the words that someone says to you "out of the blue." You might get a $20 rebate, a credit note, or an unexpected gift. Accept these gifts and recognize them as part of your new groove. Most patterns or beliefs that you've invested in for the past 10 to 20 years will not simply disappear in a few months, even if you are diligent and hopeful. Remember that any unpleasant, painful money symptoms that arise during this time are the remnants of your past thoughts. The outer world needs time to catch up with your new thoughts. It could take some time before your thoughts meld with your reality, but it could also take an instant—it all depends on what you choose to accept.

Becoming Wireless

Our society is moving from land line telephones (hard-wired) that fix us in one position with limited movement, to cellular phones that enable the freedom of movement. This technology is made possible through radio frequencies that bounce signals between linked satellites. In order to send a message at any time, depending on your location, the combination of networks a wireless phone signal must touch could be numerous and they could differ each time you dial. As we start to find our new groove, being wired to any old belief will feel limiting, like talking on a hard-wired phone. Being hard-wired to long-held beliefs, even after all of your rewiring, stems from the idea that there is only one way of accomplishing a task. If I told you that I have $100K for you, your mind might go through any number of beliefs before it accepts what I've said and takes action. You have to stop telling yourself, "I'm no good with money," and you must begin to say, "I am brilliant at managing money!" Convincing yourself that you have acquired new skills and abilities to create whealth will take time, but pretty soon, if a positive statement in replayed in your brain, it will resonate, becoming part of the record that is your new groove. Eventually you will be, perhaps unwittingly, forming new, positive perceptions of your self-worth, leaving behind those old, negative ones. It is this *holding pattern* that creates new wires. You may be satisfied with your wires, but remaining open to new ideas and possibilities will only enhance your financial-health. Have you ever said to yourself that you would like to do or have something, forgotten about it, then mentioned it to someone or picked up a newspaper only to find the very thing you wanted, at the right price and in the right colour? Somehow, it just came to you, without effort! Well, it's because you weren't wired; you had no fixed idea about how it should've come to you.

A Wireless Experience

About eight months ago my mother and I decided to buy a rental property together. It was tough for me because I had just emerged from bankruptcy and this created many hurdles, even in a booming real-estate market. We decided to improve my credit first and take a stab at it a few months later. Buying a rental property still remained a goal, but we put it on the back burner. About eight months later my mother was talking with a friend (who knew nothing of her desire to enter the real estate market). This friend mentioned that her daughter and son-in-law were moving and wanted to sell one of their rental properties. The price was within my mother's budget, and it came to us without struggle. We weren't hard-wired to any belief of how we should have entered this market. Both my mother and I were connected to the many networks that revolve around us, connections that we often don't even know exist. Still don't believe me? My eleven-year-old daughter wrote down on a piece of paper that she wanted to have $30 in a week. I was skeptical because she was only getting $20 a month for her allowance. In my adult-like fashion I asked her how she planned to accomplish this goal, and of course she didn't know. It was forgotten, but two weeks later she was given a gift certificate for her birthday. This gift didn't come in the form I had envisioned, or believed possible, and it didn't even come from me. I think that because we are all connected, a gift can come from anyone, anywhere. Mission accomplished. When you liberate yourself from the wires, you move through several stages, from believing to trusting to knowing. Trust in yourself, in your ideas and your creations, is the next challenge you face on this journey.

Chapter Three
You, Inc.

What are you worth? Do you even know? At this moment, if you're familiar with the traditional net worth statement you're probably calculating the value of your house, your savings account, and everything else you possess in order to come up with a number, right? Believe it or not, the "real world" meaning of this question, "What are you worth?" is more than a mere figure. Remember the story of how I effortlessly secured my first client? Well, my battle for financial health wasn't over then. When I first started I was asked to give a quote for what the job would cost. I agonized over how much I should charge. I had decided on $65 an hour, but when it came time to give the quote, I almost choked on the price. That'll be a s-s-seven hu-hu-hundred dollar job. I was disgusted with myself. Now when I hear the question, "What are you worth?" I know it really means, "Are you fully aware of your value and are you willing to stand by that value?" Clearly, I wasn't. I was still blocked by old beliefs and I had to do more work before I could reconfigure my net worth.

Accounting books tell us that we can calculate our net worth by first adding up the value of our assets (stocks, bonds, mutual funds, RRSPs, jewelry, real estate) and then subtracting this amount from our total liabilities (what you owe in loans and other obligations).

Our net worth is the value remaining, positive or negative. Although it does help to know the value of your net worth in its traditional sense, I would like to propose an alternate perspective of net worth.

You, Inc.

You are your greatest asset. Period. Let's look at what you own and what can be invested: there is your time, your knowledge, any of your positive qualities, your money, your reputation, your experience, your passion, and your desire. (This is just to name a few.) If you distribute these assets wisely, you will always receive a significant return on any investment. Begin by investing in financial knowledge. For example, teach your children about financial concepts, take the time to ask questions whenever you are making a financial decision, invest your time wisely, accept more, ask for more, and invest in a support system (friends and family). These investments will reap rewards and your assets will continue to grow.

One of the most important things you can do is to invest in your ideas. Ideas, or know-how, is what drives our economic progress. Innovations in science and technology save both time and money. As individuals we can economize in similar ways. Your bright ideas can bring you many rewards because there are things that only you know how to do. You might know of the best apples and preparation methods for a particular baby sauce that is gentle on an infant's digestive system. I have a good friend who was a lawyer in her own country. She married and divorced young. When she arrived in Canada she married an abusive man and divorced again. She lost faith, but after going through a women's shelter, she got back on her feet. Slowly, she started believing that she could return to school and get her law degree. As I write this, she is now in her fifties, has passed her exams, and is now waiting for news of her acceptance. Her goal is to bring to law her unique perspective as an immigrant in order to help other women avoid abusive relationships during the process of naturalization. Whatever the idea, be sure to honour it, and begin to allow it to make money for you. When you begin cultivating your ideas, you begin creating multiple streams of income for yourself, and you begin working less for your money by having your ideas work more for you.

When I awoke from my financial slumber I saw that if I made even a tiny investment in a home that I could reduce my taxes, and if my corporation bought the property, I could reduce my taxes even further. I also left a bank that gave me only a paltry 0.5% on my savings, charged me for ATM / Interac transactions, charged me $12.95 a month for service charges, *and* $5 for transfer fees. Now, I'm with bank that gives me 3% on savings, $0 ATM / Interac transaction fees, no service charges, and $0 for transfers! When I was laid off I was receiving unemployment and I put away $20 a month to create my own over-draft account draft account of $100 at 0% interest! In short, I took the time to invest in who I was and where I wanted to go. I found that I began to think differently about myself as I took control of my finances. I realized that I was a financially capable person.

Belief in the I'm-possible

For a company to work together (to-get-there), the entire company must "buy-in," or strike an agreement, whenever implementing new policies of directions. If company heads don't have buy-in, it could mean that a greater degree of effort must be exerted when trying to sell the idea internally to its staff. Before you achieve financial-health you must come to an understanding with close family members and friends (to-get-there).

Is it possible for me to earn one million dollars? Is it possible for me to feel happy about money—no matter how much, or how little I have in my wallet that day? Could I possibly believe that there will always be enough, in spite of my current circumstances? Is it possible that my writing will be of interest to other people? Will it help people? Is it possible for me to move out of this tiny apartment and into a larger home? We must have faith and we must believe in what is seemingly impossible: poverty can be eradicated and whealth can be achieved. We can find ways to eliminate crime, and we can produce strong, compassionate leaders for every generation. If I don't believe in myself, how can I believe in humanity? Believing in the I'm-possible means turning away from the limited and opening the door to the limitless. It means giving up the illusion of lack and scarcity and looking at abundance and prosperity.

Recently, I went to a seminar that consisted of about 150 people, and although the room was packed, everyone was in a good mood. The speaker asked if we'd like to learn something interesting about our beliefs surrounding money, and we responded, "Yeah, sure." He took $100 from his pocket and handed the bills to an attendee so the amount could be confirmed. Then, holding up the bills he asked, "Who in here will give me $50 for this $100?" The room went silent. Finally, one brave soul stood, took out a $50, and gave it to the speaker. In turn, the speaker handed him the $100. Our mouths hung open. No one could believe it, and then we were all berating ourselves. The man who had made the trade, buying himself $100 for $50, had trust. His belief in I'm-possible was stronger than his fears about looking like a fool, failing, or losing. The speaker asked why the rest of us did not accept his offer. The majority of the room admitted that they didn't trust his offer; they thought it was a scam, or they were afraid of looking like idiots. It seemed that everyone, with exception of one person, lacked faith, or trust. When we trust someone or something, we believe in the power of transformation, and we do not doubt. We didn't trust that the speaker was making a legitimate offer. We didn't believe in ourselves. In other words, we didn't "buy in." Essentially, this is the root of any financial breakdown. After that night, I trusted myself to walk around with $1,000 in my wallet. I no longer thought that I would spend it, or lose it, or that someone would steal my money. I even started to believe that I could support myself financially, and that one day soon I would make wise financial decisions. The process of healing begins with trusting yourself, even if this trust is incrementally gained, a little at a time. We've become so used to trusting other people's opinions and disregarding our own. We must banish this old habit and learn to trust our own judgements; we have to be realistic with ourselves and cultivate our own money management philosophy. This is how we will gain mastery over our money. Expert opinions, gurus, consultants, and portfolio managers are all fine, and they serve a purpose, but now it's time to reclaim the throne of self-trust, and believe in the I'm-possibility of creating and sustaining your own concepts of whealth. It's a simple plan and an innocent first step.

Damage Control

For anyone who's ever been through bankruptcy or a serious financial crisis, repairing or restoring credit is of major concern. Implementing habits that will maintain a clean credit record is vital to the re-establishment of financial-wellness. Rarely is this an easy feat, and no one wants to make it easy. Hey, you've failed in your obligations to repay debts, so why should anyone take a chance on you now? Did you know that applying for credit more than six times a year actually hurts your credit? Also, applying for and receiving credit in more than three places can also negatively impact your credit record. And did you know that the FICO Beacon Score allows businesses free access to your credit rating? This score does not show on your credit report unless you request it. For example, a bank may require a minimum score of 700 to give you a loan, whereas a car dealer looking to give you a lease may only need a score of 500. Knowledge is power. Knowing the contents of your credit report is very important to financial-health. Perhaps the most frustrating aspect of regaining credit after bankruptcy is the fact that the only way to re-establish credit is to create new debt, thereby showing a consistent, positive payment history. That's why it's important to first focus on inner financial-health, and then on credit repair or restoration. When you emerge from bankruptcy you know your credit report will likely be poor for five to seven years, but do you know the facts? About six months after bankruptcy discharge, I discovered that five of the creditors that were originally included in my bankruptcy were still listed outside of the bankruptcy on my credit report. This was hurting my credit because it was falsely showing that even though I had declared bankruptcy, I was still continuing bad payment habits with five companies. The credit bureau was misinformed, and in turn, they were misinforming any company that had recently checked my credit. I quickly filed a complaint with a government agency and had them investigate. About 24 hours after speaking with the government agent, I received a call from one of North America's largest credit bureaus. The agent apologized, saying my report would be immediately amended and that she would send out a new credit file, not only to me but also to any company that had inquired into my credit history over the past six months! She also left me a number that I could reach her at in case I had any other problems. Your credit report is like your own public relations department. It relays information about you to the public, to anyone considering giving you credit, and it's the PR department's responsibility (your responsibility) to clean up any communication errors. After a bankruptcy, I recommend that you check your credit report every six months for the first two years, and then once every year for three years thereafter. Knowledge is power, so arm yourself with knowledge. Stay aware and be ready and willing to take action.

Chapter Four
Asking, Expecting, Accepting

Visualization is the beginning of all healing. There is an art and science to seeing beyond the minutiae of what is in front of us. What you are looking at now is part of your past. It is the result of something you've thought of in the before, be it a minute, an hour, or a year ago. Whether you're holding a coffee cup, a pen, or a baby, this reality is the result of a thought you've had before. Because the act of thinking naturally becomes automated, thoughts seem to happen so quickly that we don't recognize we've had them *before* the act. Now, let's slow things down a little in order to speed things up. A paradox, I know, but get used to it because life is full of them. Visualization is a practice that requires slowing down, and in this act we take control so that we can become the author, painter, and architect of our lives again. It seems like a slow process because it's like being taught how to ride a bike when you've been doing it for 30 years. The consequences of visualization can be likened to a moment of grace, like when you finally put all of the elements of riding a bike together: desire, focus, balance... you were off! With visualization-or seeing different- ly—it's the same. You calm your breathing, focus (on finan- cial-health), ignite your desire, and balance your fears and doubts with love and trust.

How do you see your financial-health? Do you see yourself with more than enough? What are you doing with it? How are you investing it? How is it supporting your values? How are you sharing it? How is it making you happy? Notice the thoughts that arise and any bodily sensations that are released as you begin to *see*... There are five ingredients to healing your financial life through visualization. These elements are to ask, to visualize, to expect, to act, and to let go. Let's look at a very simple exercise that makes use of all five ingredients. By following these steps, you will become more comfortable with the process of visualization. First, I want you to get comfortable. (Make sure you are rested and in a relatively positive mood.) 1. (Ask) Focus on an aspect of your financial life that you would like to improve. I want you to contemplate this for a few minutes. 2. (Visualize) Picture yourself enjoying perfect health in this area. Experience it with all five senses. Visualize yourself touching whatever is in this scene...smell it...taste it... 3. (Expect) Stay with this moment, and tell yourself that you enjoy this peace and tranquility. Tell yourself that you are worthy and that you deserved to succeed in this arena. Do this without any doubt. 4. (Act) Now take initiative. Whatever it is that you need to do in order to begin living this vision, even in the smallest way, do it. Trust it. Act with integrity and gratitude. 5. (Let Go) This moment belongs to you, so it is yours to let go. You own this creation and it is yours. It is time to start new, and now that you have freed yourself of this old worry, you can begin again. Forgive yourself and move on.

Handling the Flow

The subconscious mind is always active. This is why it helps to create a want list. Like its name suggests, a "want list" includes everything you want, no matter how frivolous. Go ahead, be bold, ask for whatever you want: big, small, ridiculous, outrageous, seemingly impossible, even characteristics you wish to adopt can go on the want list. Next, beside each want write down the quality, or feeling you expect to have when you possess each item. What will you gain from having this item or quality? Write this answer in a colour other than black or blue ink. For example, if I want a trip to France, the quality I am trying to acquire is freedom and expansion. At night, while you sleep, the subconscious conjures ways to bring you what you have asked for, whether it be a quality or an object. You will see that things "happen" almost without effort. Our subconscious has a link to unknown, higher powers, and to every other living being on the planet as well. At this point we do not concern ourselves with *how* the subconscious works, we simply trust that it will provide.

This exercise is important for three reasons: it gets us to go back to ourselves, to our connection, to the Source. Here, we find what we want instead of paying attention to things like the credit cards, banks, stores, and the affections of others. Secondly, it gets us in touch with the bigger picture, giving us a sense of what's behind it all, making us more aware and in control of our own urges. Finally, by asking we are creating a receptacle for money because we have attracted it and it needs to go

Source

Source is our own divine connection with the Creative, call it God, It, Allah, Buddha—whatever. Source is our link to this infinite ocean from which everything springs. Our source can never be lost. We may forget it's there, but it's never lost.

somewhere.

Money needs to move around and be in motion. Money needs to play. So, the want list helps us play with money. We have become much too serious about money and we need to lighten up. A want list helps us distribute our whealth wisely and joyfully, even before it arrives. When it does arrive, it's important to acknowledge receipt by saying "thank you." You may also find that you receive the thing you wanted and this thing may not involve money. Be certain to say "thanks" for this gift too. I worked with one of my clients on this and the saddest thing was that it took this client almost three months to create a list of no more than five things. He was so afraid to ask, let alone accept the goodness waiting for him. Gradually he started adding to the list, but even as I write this he still has no more than ten items on his list. It is vital that when you write this list, you must prepare your state of mind to receive a gift in whatever way it presents itself to you. You may receive it as a deep discount on an item, or you could receive it as a birthday gift, an insight, a compliment. Prepare yourself to accept these gifts in any way, shape, or form.

Ask-Expect-Accept

It is my belief that financially-whealthy people expect and accept more from life. The whealthy automatically ask-expect-accept, as opposed to someone in ill financial-health, who will normally follow the pattern of worry-block-refuse. I have found that the financially healthy *ask* for more than the poor. They *expect* the best, and they *accept* things when they do arrive. They don't even realize they are doing it and they've never stopped to think about the process. This process, ask-expect-accept, is automatic within the financially healthy. Where did they learn it? Were they born with it? Did they adopt it? How can we learn to make this process automatic within ourselves?

When I was growing up there was a poem hanging on

the wall of our den entitled "Children Learn What They Live" by Desiderata. In the poem, children modelled themselves after their parents by watching how their parents behaved. While many financially-healthy people may have seen their parents worry about money, it is likely that the ask-accept-expect pattern was far more prevalent than the worry-doubt-refuse pattern. This goes much deeper than seeing your parents, or influential individuals, handle money wisely or unwisely. The people who handle their money well as adults have continually *allowed themselves* to ask, *felt* the expectation, and, as children, have *witnessed* an acceptance of abundance. Often, when you open up this valve of ask-expect-accept, it releases forces that seem overwhelming or unwanted. It feels like you've opened up a Pandora's Box, but you must keep going.

Ghosts, Goblins and Things That Go Bump in the Night and Day

Guilt and fear—of which doubt is an offspring—are the biggest inhibitors of financial whealth that I know of. Worry, guilt, and fear are other techniques we use to scare ourselves into remaining on the debt treadmill. Worry is a disease that causes us to make negative predictions about the future and it can create negative outcomes—I recall many nights that I spent awake in bed thinking about how I wanted to join Toastmasters and better my public speaking skills. I'd visualize the date I wanted to start, think about my limited funds, and say to myself, "There's no way that I'll have enough money by then! I won't have enough leftover after paying the bills." I was projecting fear and worry onto a future possibility, telling myself it could never happen! Talk about sabotage—a proven recipe for creating more anxiety and failure. We often shy away from the things that frighten us, but we have to face the things we fear if we are to conquer them. Our fears show themselves in many different forms and they plague us at all hours of the day and night. Incessant and silent, our worries eat away at our supply of energy: "Will we have enough to put our kids through university or college? Can I really take that trip? Will we ever have enough for a new house? So and so's birthday is approaching... will we have enough for a gift?" Some monsters can be slain, while others can only be tamed. And yes, they can seem like gigantic creatures, but since we created them, we can also eradicate these unruly beasts. And come they will, once you open the door to accepting more. Are you going to fight these monsters with your bare hands? No. You need an effective set of tools or weapons. Your past experiences have given you a toolbox; let's look inside to see which unique tools you have gained over time.

Tool One - Checking-In

Checking-in keeps you in touch with how you're responding to the changes you're making. Checking-in also allows you to make any necessary adjustments in a timely fashion. Above all, checking-in clarifies what direction you are moving in.

Try answering these questions before going to bed at night:

1. Progress: What results have I seen from my actions today?
2. What do I want? What is the step I'm working on now?
3. What am I willing to do for this goal? Could I accept it now?
4. What is my *now* feeling about this goal?
5. What is my top priority for the next day?
6. What is my motivation? What is my purpose for action?
7. What do I see now that the goal is accomplished? How do I feel?
8. Is this goal still in alignment with my Greater Purpose?
9. Name ten things that I'm most grateful for now.
10. What is my goal for this week?

After just a few short days of doing this exercise before bed, you will find yourself having greater clarity about where you are and why you're doing what it is you're doing. The next day will run much more smoothly.

Tool Two - Listen

Ask for what you want and then listen. Listening helps us navigate through the darkness, and most of us are still afraid of the dark, or the unknown. If you think of the darkness as being like a womb, you will begin to understand that the darkness is where ideas and innovative solutions are born. You can listen with your whole body, with your eyes, your ears, your pallet, your touch, and even with your dreams. You may find that what you've asked for really is not for you, that you really don't want it, or that your body, or spirit might come to reject it if you do accept it. I'll show you what I mean by this: at one time I decided to build a Web site. As the site was being built I never had any doubts about the usefulness and the need for the service. I was receiving expertise from another person who had co-originated the idea with me, but who was not willing to put any funds into the company. In the beginning, I budgeted and was prepared to pay about $700 for the site, but as this person kept suggesting different things—and as I kept agreeing to the changes—the expense slowly grew until it totalled about $1,500! Intuitively, I knew that something was wrong because my body was always restless when I thought about the site. I started having doubts. I realized that I wasn't listening to my inner voice. I wasn't taking control of my creation. I was waiting for someone "more knowledgeable" to save me. Thankfully, I halted all of the unimportant areas of the site, mark them as "coming soon," and I focused my attention (and the Web site creator's attention) on the two areas of greatest importance. I informed the other person of my decision and he agreed with me wholeheartedly. This relieved us both of a lot of pressure. This is why it's important to be aware of the *quality* of the thing you are asking for. Focus on the quality of the thing you are asking for, and with it will come greater attributes than you could have ever imagined.

Many of our beliefs about asking are embedded in our concepts of God and our relationship with this Source. Many of us believe we are unworthy of happiness, that we are undeserving, and that we are taking away from others when we do receive. We have to believe that we are worthy of receiving. If we are patient, open, and accepting, we will receive more than enough. Use the listening tool to get closer to the things you really want so that you do not waste any time.

Tool Three - Accept Outside Help

Lately the big thing in business is outsourcing, which is the hiring of outside help. Generally, a company will outsource the projects that are not its core service or product. Outsourcing saves time and it allows a company to focus on what's most important (their "bottom line"). Individuals in financial crisis need to outsource, or seek outside help. There are many ways to do this; you may want to consult with a financial planner, seek credit counseling or speak with a close friend. When I was going through bankruptcy there were many hurdles I had to overcome before I could achieve financial-health. I sought the help of a therapist, read many books on financial planning and investing, and picked the brains of successful real estate professionals. I knew I couldn't do it alone, I knew I didn't have all the answers, but I did know that I wanted to leave my place of need and rise into prosperity.

Tool Four - Service

When we shift our attention away from our own problems, matters are put into their *proper* perspectives: you're missing a month of rent—not a limb or a child; you've had to use your child's college fund to bail yourself out of a financial crisis—not to pay the medical bills of a terminally ill family member. Volunteering is a very important tool because it connects us to many people and it allows us to cultivate compassion for other individuals. This kind of mindfulness energizes us because we are no longer focusing upon, or overanalyzing our own predicaments. The rich volunteer and donate their time to help raise awareness or money for those in need. Why wait until you have money in your hand. Aren't you whealthy right now? Get out there and do something for someone other than yourself, even if you have kids and are struggling to make ends meet. Get involved, and get your family involved too! This is a very powerful tool because it lets you meet other people who are influential, who've already made it, and you can network with them. Give (while you're asking) and you'll receive so much more!

Tool Five - See a Penny, Count a Blessing

We see pennies all the time...on the road, in the coffee shop, in our purse, in the car, on the floor....you always see them, right? Next time you see a penny, count a blessing. It could be anything: you're grateful that you have a car, or you're grateful that you have a $10 in your pocket. You must repeat these blessings and be thankful for what you do own. Use the pennies to not only remind you of the whealth you are working towards, but also of the whealth you already possess.

Tool Six - Let It Go

Imagine a typical morning scene: you've just finished eating your morning cereal, you walk to the kitchen sink to deposit the spoon and bowl. Does the spoon and bowl stick to your hand? Do you have to force yourself to put them down? No, you don't. You set them down easily and effortlessly. Naturally, you weren't worried about the sink shifting out of your reach, or about your inability to set these items down. Right? Then why do we have such a hard time letting go of our money worries? Do you think worrying will miraculously fix the problem? Creating solutions to problems requires a clear and open being. Worry is not a super fertilizer that hastens the growth of solutions. Whatever you ask for, let it go, and don't worry about how it will come to you because this is not your concern. Just ask, write it down, and let it go.

These are only six tools that allowed me to heal my financial wounds. You will likely discover some of your own tools as you journey towards whealth. These six tools will provide a foundation, however, and I urge you to incorporate them into your daily life. Some days, you might rely on tools one, two, and five; on other days, you might need to practice three, four, and six. They all work, but the combination of tools you might need to use will depend on both internal and external forces.

Chapter Five

Greater Purpose

What is Greater Purpose? The best way that I can put it is this: Greater Purpose is your reason for being on this planet. When your ship has sails, you can direct it. When Greater Purpose has you, your energy and your actions have meaning, and you are aware of that meaning. When Greater Purpose finds you, you see that nothing you have gone through is meaningless, redundant, or wasted—no matter how painful, humiliating, or sad. All of this is a type of organic fertilizer. When you become aware of Greater Purpose in your life, even your money takes on new meaning because you will be attracting it for a reason. Money will come alive to you in new ways, illuminating all corners of your imagination. Your Greater Purpose, what only you can do in this world, will nourish you, and it will clothe you if you let it. It satisfies. When you look hard enough and find the thing you were meant to do, it usually brings greater awareness, goodness, and gifts to more than just yourself. A mother who believes her Greater Purpose in life is to aid her children in becoming compassionate, responsible individuals may not realize that she is inspiring the other mothers she meets in the park. Greater Purpose always involves the lives of many. There is a level of consciousness, or knowing, involved with Greater Purpose because it entails seeing beyond. When you are engaged in any act, you can see at the same time how the outcome of the event can help others.

The whealthy always try to leave a legacy, while the

poor only try to get by. Unfortunately, the poor must expend a good deal of their energy on the struggle of day-to-day existence. Legacies are part of our Greater Purpose. They inspire others to greatness, and ignite the imagination, whether we are aware of it or not. Before I was inspired to write this book I was very much in debt. I owed almost $60,000—after bankruptcy. The humiliation and guilt that I endured for years was enormous and I felt heavier with each passing day. To make matters worse, I was laid off a few months before, and I was beginning to throw myself into another business venture. I felt as if I would live in my tiny apartment for the rest of my life, but something within me wanted to share my experiences so that others could learn from my journey. Greater Purpose usually grows out of adversity and turbulence. British barons drafted the Magna Carta, the document on which the Declaration of Independence is based, and this charter arose from the outrage over increasing taxation at the hands of greedy kings. South Africa's independence, and the world's increased awareness of the right of individual freedom, grew from one person's Greater Purpose. Whole hospital wings and universities are donated by the whealthy in dedication to their beloved deceased, out of sorrow and their longing. These actions ignite greater awareness and the desire to help others. This demonstrates that any adversity can contribute to your Greater Purpose. Have you always struggled with poor health and are now experiencing a renewal? Are you doing your best to overcome poverty, having faced multiple challenges? Were you fighting an addiction that you've found release and meaning from? Or, maybe you are a single parent who is succeeding, even in the face of adversity? There are always situations that you have handled in an effective way. Many people are fighting with these very issues and you could have something of value to contribute to their lives. These things are what the recipes of Greater Purpose are made of.

They are there not only for you to learn and grow from, but also for you to share with others. The ways in which you overcome your adversities are uniquely your own, and no one else could have come up with those solutions. Sharing can be as simple as talking with a group, if the topic comes up, or it can be writing an article, a book, painting, or starting a non-profit organization that heightens people's understanding of whealth.

Life on Purpose and the Art of Extraction

One thing we have to do is overcome our fear of Greater Purpose. I remember taking an art class, and asking the instructor why I was having difficulty with a drawing. I would get to a place where I really liked what I was drawing, and then I'd hit a wall of fear. I was afraid of continuing because I was afraid of failing. My instructor smiled and said she wished she was the type of teacher who would force me to tear up my work—every single piece—even the work I was proud of. What do you mean, *rip it up?!* "Yes," she said, "if I were tough enough I would make you destroy every single piece of work that you've ever done so that you might stop becoming so attached to what you've created in the past. This way, you might focus on each *present piece,* and on the new skills you are currently learning." My instructor didn't have the courage to make me do it over, again and again and again. Life, however, forces us to improve upon our creations; over and over, life will destroy the things we cherish, again and again. Surely, on more than one occasion you've noticed yourself going through the same experiences, almost in circles: people you love dearly are always using the exit door; money seems to come and quickly go. Each time you experience hardship, you either gain more fear, or you let it go and make room for happiness. Life will tear up your drawings, so you have to remember, it isn't the drawing that's important, rather, it's what you learn from drawing and how you share your art with the world that makes all the difference. Until you let go of the fears and embrace your Greater Purpose, you'll keep going in circles and your creations will be torn apart. Many of us are afraid that if we give ourselves to Greater Purpose that we will feel unfulfilled, that our identities will somehow get lost in its greatness with less control. The truth is that we will be given more than enough and we'll become even greater beings with increased control over our lives. Don't be afraid of your mistakes. They are the ingredients in your recipe for Greater Purpose.

There is a technique used in art that teaches a student to first draw the dominant lines of any given shape. Dominant lines are the lines of an object that your eyes are immediately drawn to. A dominant area will guide you so that you know what to draw, or how far or how close you need the next line to be in order to complete the object. Let your own dominant lines guide you through life: trust your strongest character traits and follow your desires; pay attention to the recurring themes in your life because these will enable you to define your Greater Purpose. When you are learning to draw objects in art, one circle isn't enough; you need to practice drawing many shapes, and eventually, out of those many shapes, a form or pattern will evolve. The point is, it takes several shapes to create a pattern, just like it will take several experiences to shape your Greater Purpose. Your Purpose will become visible after many recurring (shapes) events, and when it finally hits you, you will exclaim, "AHA!"

Another way to draw—and draw out your Greater Purpose—is to take the focus off of the object itself and start looking at the space around the object. In other words, it can be easier to identify your Greater Purpose if you are not looking *directly* at your life, but at the things around you. For example, violence in your teen's high school might trigger a desire to work with troubled teens. Perhaps you might notice a rise in the number of people afflicted with colds and so you decide to educate people about nutrition. You get the drift, right?

It's now time to ask yourself these questions which will help clarify your Greater Purpose:

1. What have been some of my biggest mistakes?
2. What mistakes do I keep repeating over and over?
3. How can I share my insights?
4. What would I like my Greater Purpose to be?
5. What am I beginning to notice more of in my daily activities?
6. If you think you've found it, what is your Declaration of Greater Purpose?

When you extract, or draw out, you bring forth what you have within, and you learn to control the energy it takes to replicate form, either as an idea or an object. When you have achieved this, you will begin to live a life of Purpose, and financial-health will follow.

The reason why I use examples from drawing and art is so that I can clearly exemplify the interconnectedness of all actions; in this world, nothing is separate from anything else. Finding Greater Purpose lets you see the big picture of your life. Finding Greater Purpose also opens up your field of acceptance—and remember what I said earlier—the purpose of creating a want list is so that your money has a place to go, and to draw more money to you. It is the same with Greater Purpose. Once you expand your playing field, more will come your way. Letting Greater Purpose guide you will relieve many pressures because before you had its direction, it was like trying to paint a very tiny portrait with a very wide brush. No wonder we feel frustrated a lot of the time.

My Story

After I was discharged from bankruptcy, I was still in debt and I owed many people money. To cheer myself up, I decided that I wanted to contribute to my community by reaching out to high-school students. I chose to start a non-profit organization to help them realize their intra/entrepreneurial potential through a business plan competition. We began as five women. In our pilot year we raised over $1,500, enrolled seven kids in the project, and found summer jobs for four of them in high-tech companies—one of the kids was even called back for a second year by his employer. In our first official year, our enrollment grew from 7 to 17. Our initiative began flashing on the radar screen of some university professors who were organizing an entrepreneurial boot camp. They wanted to partner with us. I ended up sitting down with two of the directors from this program, and we mapped out how we could all collaborate in order to make this project an even greater success.

Entrepreneurship had always been a recurring thread in my life. My ventures have not always been successful, but I couldn't carve this trait out of myself even if I tried, so I have accepted it as part of my Greater Purpose. Now I have access to different kinds of people: people who aren't struggling to make ends meet, people who have whealth, people who create opportunity and have a vision.

Finding Greater Purpose brings meaning to your life and to the life of your money. It's important to realize that your money is not separate from you. Money is a direct extension of you and how you use it is indicative of your sense of self-worth. The money you make must bring meaning to your life. Sure you want a lot of money, but what for? What part of you will it really enhance? I'm not saying that wanting money to purchase real estate is not a noble or worthy cause, but there must be meaning behind each purchase. Your relationship with money must reach beyond "the accumulation of more;" you must be mindful of the decisions you make, and the abundance they bring must, first and foremost, nurture your internal whealth. If a seemingly fruitful venture seems too risky, is it worth the stress? Do you desire more money because you want to learn how to handle more? You want to learn how to manage your own estate? Do you want to know what it's like to have the freedom to purchase whatever you want? Do you want to feel a sense of getting to the next level, getting out of the fishbowl? Whatever the deeper meanings behind your desire might be, get to know the driving forces that direct your financial decisions. This will provide the springboard for your plunge into outer whealth.

Becoming Whole

You will accomplish whealth if this is what you truly want. You will find it within yourself and you will attract those who can help you to achieve whealth. Starting from

Greater Purpose is about starting from the pieces that are already in your life. I was once told to begin something the way I wanted it to end up. I wanted financial-health so I imagined what I might do if I had abundant whealth. I observed people who'd achieved great whealth and this became my starting point. Doing things like starting a foundation, volunteering, investing in real estate, cultivating greater financial awareness, worrying less about outcomes, bettering my financial preparedness, and surrounding myself with like-minded individuals gave me my start. If you start where you want to end up, you accept the painting as being complete and all you have to do is connect the dots and fill in the colour. Of course, this is an oversimplification, but in essence this is what you are doing.

When the whealthy have accomplished all they desire they build foundations that share their whealth and they help other people achieve their desires. The whealthy are overwhelmed by the abundance they have been given and they want to share their gifts with the world. Inevitably, these foundations grow in whealth and size. Why not start here? Starting from Greater Purpose keeps everything together, as if held together by magic glue. It helps you stay focused and whole.

Beginning your journey towards financial-health from the point of Greater Purpose is an act that reinforces wholeness. When you realize that you are not separate from anyone or anything, you begin to see the unfolding of a whole new financial world. You must envision the whealth you want to obtain, and you must develop financial awareness; any *lack of knowledge* will cost you every single day. It will also cost everyone else. To better illustrate my point I'll tell you a story of something that happened to me: I was once a client at one of Canada's largest banks and I chose to subscribe to their on-line banking service as an alternative to telephone or in-person banking. I checked my account twice daily so that I could be sure that my accounts were in good order. One day I noticed a cheque had cleared, but a couple of hours later when I checked again, there was no trace of the cheque coming or going. What I did notice was a charge for insufficient funds. I called the bank's 1-800 number and after explaining the situation to a representative, he also agreed that there was enough money in the account to cover the cheque and that there was no reason why it should have been returned. What we concluded was that the bank had completely wiped clear any trace of the cheque's activity because they were afraid their bank fees would not be covered. I had him reimburse me the $20 NSF fee, and I went to my branch the next day. I was directed to speak to a personal banking manager. She said their system allowed them to see the cheque come in and go out, but that I—the customer—would not be able to view this on-line. She also said that although I may want her to say this wouldn't happen again, she said it was only going to get worse and then she implied I shouldn't be worrying anyway because the transactions would be shown on my bank statement. Well, guess what? They didn't show up on the statement! Not even a trace! I called the bank manager and she confirmed that the bank has the right to retract a transaction, but that it should be reflected on my statement *and* on-line. She said she put a "flag" into the headoffice so they could fix this glitch. This experience taught me the importance of educating myself about money matters. Do you know how much your bank is charging you for services fees? Do you know what these services include? How many ATM withdrawals and debit transactions are you allotted each month before the bank begins charging you for these transactions? How much are you being charged for using another bank's machine? How much for transfers? How much for on-line banking? What percentage are you being charged on overdraft? What are the rates of two other competing banks? If you haven't considered any of these queries, it's time you looked for the answers. Make some comparisons today!

We will continue our quest in the coming chapters, where we learn more about the development of whealth. Money has a unique energy—hence, its similarity to a current (currency), or electricity—and it needs to play and be free. Rebuilding your financial strength from the point of Greater Purpose will allow your money to flow and play in a bigger area. In the next section we will combine all of the pieces into a working whole. It's time to play!

Chapter Six

Attention

Chapter Six

Whole corporations are gathering together to figure out how to "manage" our attention because human beings tend to doze off in the middle of anything complex or confusing. Attention is the currency of the new economy. Attention is priceless. It is worth more than gold. Giving someone or something your attention is similar to giving orders to your subconscious. Your mind is like the cave where Ali Baba and his Forty Thieves held their treasures, and the door only opens upon a particular command: "Open Sesame (Open Says Me)". When you give your attention away, you open yourself up to givers and takers. Giving away your attention is similar to giving someone that special password, and often we are not discerning enough about what we give our attention to. We readily give our attention to billboards, to worries that are beyond our control, to people who do not appreciate us. Your money goes where your attention goes. Attention is a concentrated, focused energy. Ask yourself, "Where does my attention go?" Do you worry a lot about money? Do you worry about not being a good enough parent? Do you worry about not having enough, about not getting that job, that raise, or that bonus? Worry is like a house that isn't insulated; all of your energy seeps through the cracks. Do you pay attention to your financial matters, to how you're going to pay the bills? Do you focus on building a picture perfect home like the images in the magazines, or do you focus on creating the perfect "home" for yourself?

Remember, you will find your rewards in the places you pay the most attention to, so focus your energy in the right direction.

Where does your attention go? How many times did you look at your e-mail today? How much time did you spend listening to the news, or watching TV, arguing, or worrying? How much time did you spend looking at your budget, touching your money before giving it away, creatively solving a financial issue, visualizing more money, or feeling good about the money you do have? Have you spent any time giving thanks for the whealth you do own? It's time to focus on the level and quality of attention that we typically give our finances:

- negative attention—fear of consequences,
- positive attention—you are excited about an outcome, or whatever sum you possess now,
- chained—the situation was forced on you; it came as a surprise out of nowhere,
- unchained—you find an aspect of your finances interesting so you volunteer your time or you choose to learn more,
- automatic pilot—like washing dishes, many tasks aren't exciting, but you habitually complete them,
- here, now—like being in love; all of you is present and you are a willing participant.

When we embark on a new journey, we often rush headlong into fixing the problem and fail to hear the vital discourse going on between our new course of action and actions we intend to take in the future. Listening, really listening, is a tool that you are going to need to use on this journey towards financial-health. Listening will help you avoid many pitfalls along the way. And you will have pitfalls—it is best that you know this now. Be prepared. Listening helps you recognize feedback; feedback is your guide. As you navigate your attention out of the murky waters of financial turmoil try to identify the types of attention you typically give to your finances and make a commitment to modify your perceptions of money and financial reactions. You want to reach your target, so listen for feedback. The adjustments a pilot makes on a spaceship are physical (technical), but humans are complex and the areas we need to monitor and adjust are physical, emotional, and spiritual. Here are some examples of the kinds of monitoring and adjusting you may encounter on this journey:

Monitor—you get an NSF cheque
Adjust—get better acquainted with your money; it's time to create a slush fund

Monitor—a personal loan is due ahead of schedule and your friend needs the money now
Adjust—don't get mad, frustrated, or annoyed; realize that somewhere in your new committment you asked to clear up your debt and make a plan

Monitor—your bank ups their service fees
Adjust—you look around for a bank offering a better deal

Monitor—you're looking around for a house, but you keep hitting stumbling blocks
Adjust—give it time and re-evaluate; it might not be the right time

Pay Attention to Your Body (It Knows Your Truth)

The first thing we are aware of in a crisis is the pain, whether it is physical or emotional. Financial crisis causes a great deal of anxiety and this kind of stress wears on the body. You might find that you suffer from headaches, or that you often have lower back pain. These ailments could be symptomatic of the anxiety a financial crises forces you to endure. The exercise that follows will help you to listen to your body, which is always sending you messages and signals. Before you can monitor the signals and make adjustments, you must first learn how to recognize the messages your body is sending you.

Exercise:

Think about a financial fiasco that you've recently experienced. Did it really upset you? Recall it and relive it in its entirety. Where are you feeling the pain? Where is that crisis making itself known to you? Is it your back, your shoulders, your head, or your skin? Recognize it and file it away, but remember that it needs to be sorted out. You could get off track if you continue to ignore it further. So, from now on when you find yourself clenching your teeth with worry, you can ask "Am I reacting to a financial worry?" If so, you can then monitor it and make the necessary mental and physical adjustments.

Pay Attention to Your Thoughts

What we allow to run through our minds about money on a minute-to-minute basis will play a large role in our financial-health. When you encounter a financial crisis, what typically runs through your mind? Perhaps something like—"I'm such a loser!; I knew this couldn't last; I'll never be rich because life is against me." It seems that I've always been afraid of money and this fear has always clouded my thoughts. I saw my parents fight over money, and I've seen others suffer from having too little money. We all know that money can cause rifts and that people have allowed it to destroy many good relationships. For a long time, I saw money as the enemy: an insurmountable beast that I expected would fail me, hurt me, exclude me, and humiliate me. There were many times when my financial blunders did, in fact, humiliate me. Once, when I was in the middle of changing banks I wrote a cheque to my doctor and it bounced because of a bank error. I reimbursed my doctor and some time later when I purchased more remedies from her by cheque, the cheque bounced again. I received a call from my doctor's assistant and I was told that I had to pay by cash from now on. Shamed and humiliated, I called my new bank and they admitted that they had made an error. They apologized and reimbursed me the NSF charge that I had incurred. I called the assistant to let her know that it was not my fault, but she remained uncaring and cold. I tried to tell myself that it was not my fault. I tried to be gentle with myself, but I continued to beat myself up. Destructive thought patterns are very hard to break. The lack of respect I had for myself was often reflected in the ways other people treated me. Perhaps people sensed my vulnerability and therefore thought they could treat me as harshly as I treated myself. We are often unkind to ourselves and what we must realize is that any act of self-deprecation must stop if we are to embrace whealth and see ourselves as being worthy of more.

For every action there is an equal and opposite reaction, and what many of us fail to grasp is that thinking is an action that precedes any bodily reaction. Yes, we react to our thoughts. By berating myself I was only perpetuating more of the actions that I did not want. I did not make any room in my mind for that financially responsible person I knew I could become because I believed that I was incapable of managing a mere $100. Now, I am much kinder to myself. Now, I can manage $10,000. I allow room for error and growth. I visualize where I want to be and I constantly encourage myself. You might not believe it, but being kind to yourself does make a difference to your pocketbook. Do you feel more generous towards a person who growls at you when asking for money, or to someone who asks kindly? Within your world, you need to construct an inviting internal atmosphere for whealth.

Life has taught me many lessons and one thing I

learned from my string of financial crises was that I always need to do a lot of listening. I held erroneous beliefs that needed to be heard and corrected. In my daily interactions, life let me know that I still had work to do. I was given feedback that I could monitor, and I didn't deny it, push it away, or reject it. This feedback could be how terribly a bank employee treated me, or it could be the way the doctor's assistant treated me over the bounced cheque. When we reject the information given to us, whether it comes in the form of blame, guilt, or anger, we aren't "paying" attention and eventually we end up paying a much greater price. If we ignore our issues with money, there will be negative financial repercussions. If I didn't listen, I would have misplaced my priorities, my energies; I would have started juggling money all over the place, frantically trying to rectify the error as soon as possible. Instead, as in the case of my bounced cheques, I took a minute to monitor the feedback and I gave it the attention it deserved—that I deserved. Remember, it is essential that you reflect before you react.

Pay Attention to Your Outer Circumstances

We are all in this together. We are all connected to each other; take comfort in this thought. One of my best friends has been living with financial crisis all of her life. As a single mother, my friend has experienced many financial constraints, and she has never been able to get a solid financial hold on her life. Her sense of self-worth has always been slight, and she often finds herself living with others because she can't find enough money for first and last month's rent. She spends generously on others because she is unwilling to face the facts of her financial situation. She's not listening to her feedback; she's in denial. When reality comes knocking on her door, she's unprepared. Unfortunately, my friend will have to learn to cultivate her financial wisdom the hard way. If you listen, and pay attention to your feedback, you won't have the same difficulties as my friend. Your unique circumstances are your control panel buttons blinking on and off, and they tell you when something is amiss. You can learn a lot about your situation by monitoring how others react to you.

Mental Exercise:

Past Circumstances: Think of a situation in the past when you were embarrassed or financially hurt by someone. What circumstances led to the event? Can you recall any of the warning signs that you received during that time? Was it because you didn't listen, or because you were afraid? How did you respond to the incident? Did you make the necessary corrections after? What specific actions could you have taken to adjust the outcome?

Current Circumstances: Now think of a current financial hot potato that you are juggling right now. Maybe you're hoping a cheque didn't bounce; or you promised to repay someone, but you just spent the money and you haven't told them yet. How is life trying to tell you that this might not be the right course of action? How are you responding to life's feedback? What corrective actions could you take to set yourself back on course? Commit to completing this act!

Pay Attention to Your Input

We should always try to track the feedback that filters through our senses, even if it isn't immediately clear as to what this feedback might be telling us. Why are we astonished when we receive negative results from the junk we fill our minds with everyday? Why are we surprised when we can no longer respond adequately because our hearts and minds are malnourished? On any given day this is what many of us feed ourselves:

- we rise and feel angst over the work we have chosen,
- we contemplate, with tension, the busy day ahead (1/2 cup of anxiety),
- we drive to work and someone swerves in front of our car; we become angry (1/4 cup of anger),
- we argue with a co-worker (1/4 cup of anger),
- we gossip about a co-worker (1 cup of anger),
- we watch *Ally McBeal* and *Law & Order* (2 cups of fear),
- we watch the news (1/2 cup of fear),
- we listen to the radio with its dismal song lyrics, advertisements, etc. (1 cup of sadness mixed with fear).

Who could live on such a diet? Everyday, people sing the same song: "There's never enough." We've come to believe that we don't deserve the same happiness as others, and we are convinced that we have to guard, fight for, and lie for the things we've rightfully earned. This is why we have to focus on what's inside; we can't always control our external surroundings, and adding "more stuff" won't make any real difference. However, we can choose who and what we will invite into our lives. Be vigilant. Pay attention. You wouldn't let just anyone into your home, would you?

Chapter Seven
Financial Alchemy

Financial turmoil, especially bankruptcy, ruptures the fabric of our lives, creating a gap that inhibits our well-being. That moment of imbalance and instability, which occurs between your past and future, that critical space of Divine Possibility is where you can conduct your transformation. This is what I call financial alchemy.

Each of us engages in alchemy, either intentionally through conscious choice, or unintentionally when the pain caused by our experiences finally awakens us to greater awareness. At the heart of alchemy is the belief that each object is alive and has a life force that exists, sleeps, and waits to be born so that it can be used for some Greater Purpose. As financial alchemists, we must learn how to turn destructive, self-sabotaging actions into life-enhancing substances. In our inner laboratory we can purify our destructive money patterns and we can develop a higher source of energy. There are two forms of financial alchemy: one is the transformation of money matter—turning a little into a lot—the second is a change that happens within the alchemist, whereby a new individual emerges from the ashes of financial ruin. These are the two transformations that must take place and one will not happen without the other.

Alchemy 101

Alchemy is the ancient art of turning a base metal into a precious metal, such as lead into gold. But, "originally,

Divine Possibility

Divine Possibility is the space between thought and manifestation. Every eventuality is possible at this point until you inject your will and make a choice, which leads to a series of outcomes and choices, then finally manifestation. This space is what I call Divine Possibility. It is another place where we can connect to the unknown, or God.

alchemy was an ancient tradition of sacred chemistry used to discern the spiritual and temporal nature of reality: its structures, its laws, and its functions." A strong connection exists between the transformation of the base metals and our financial transformation. There are five elements in alchemy: Fire, Water, Air, Earth and Materia Prima (life force or essence). These elements are used in the key stages of the creation and transformation of matter. There are five key forces used to influence your financial transformation: Power of the Word, Power of Conscious Choice, Power of Conscious Thought, Power of Purposeful Action and Power of the Question. Join me in the lab as we explore these elements in greater detail.

The Power of Conscious Thought

The truth is that many of us do not have a lot of experience thinking or consciously directing our thoughts. Have you ever asked yourself if there is a better way for you to think, or whether your way of thinking could be effective or not? Do you ever suspect that your thinking is the primary contributor to your financial demise?

We all have our own system of analysis when confronted with a situation that needs to be resolved. Our own unique set of post-situational thoughts erupts after an incident has occurred. Most of us deal with our finances by asking, "Now what?" Often, we don't question our decisions until *after* the $500 dress has been bought; *after* the $3,000 commission has been spent and can't even be accounted for; *after* we've written several cheques only to find that we're overdrawn and have incurred an NSF charge; *after* we've been laid off and we don't have any savings to help us keep afloat during the transition. If we are continually making poor financial decisions, landing ourselves in precarious positions, why don't we start thinking—carefully—before we act? Pre-situational thoughts are an investment, and they can save us a lot of grief. The next time you find yourself standing before a cashier, your cart filled with "impulse buys," stop and ask yourself, "Can I really afford this?" Our thoughts always precede our actions.

Not many of us stop to look at the way our thoughts impact our lives, or the lives of those around us. This next exercise encourages you to become more familiar with the thoughts that drive your financial choices.

Exercise:
For the next week track the thoughts you have about money. Write them down. Do you relive a time in your childhood when there wasn't enough for groceries? Or maybe it's a brief thought of not having enough next month, 3 months from now, 6 months from now. What goes through your mind when you see your shiny, new dream car, your dream home, or designer clothes in the magazines? Have you given any thought to how you want to feel about money one year from now? How you want to think about money one year from now? This is one way to train

your thoughts to be conducive to greater financial growth.

Knowing your thoughts is essential if you are going to gather your energy particles. In the distillation process of alchemy, finer substances are extracted from heavier elements. The same must be done with our thoughts if we are to liberate ourselves from undue financial pressures and lighten our mental load. Try these three exercises and see how much lighter you feel, simply because you have chosen your thoughts. If you experience difficulties, aim to finish the 3-day mental cleanse. If you find that the exercise benefits you right from the start, proceed to the 7-day mental cleanse. If you're really up for a mental challenge and want to deep cleanse, then try the 21-day mental cleanse.

Exercise: Mental Cleansing

Commit to letting only positive thoughts enter your world. In this time of cleansing you are not to be concerned with anything of a negative nature. The mind is always trying to give you new information, trying to offer suggestions, the only problem with this is that most of the suggestions we allow it to give us are the pre-programmed, pre-used ways of old habits. When a negative thought does enter, and it will, simply tell yourself "thank you for sharing but I choose to think about...(and then choose your positive thought)." In this way you are acknowledging your mind's willingness to help and you're creating a new pattern of thought. Just for clarity, thoughts of a positive nature are always loving, kind, constructive, supportive, and expansive. Negative thoughts are those of failure, shame, guilt, jealousy, condemnation, and ridicule. Negative thoughts are pessimistic and they limit your growth. I'll give you an example of how to replace negative thoughts with positive ones: I have a tendency to dwell on past failures, like when I owed my friend money that I just couldn't afford to pay when she requested it. In the past, when I recalled this instance, I would beat myself up, saying things like, "I'm so irresponsible… Why is this person still my friend?" Now, when I recall this incident, I say, "I made a mistake, but I did rectify it. I am a capable person." We have to teach ourselves how to think positively, and with enough practice, rest assured, you will develop a confidence you didn't have before.

Schedule for the 3-day mental cleanse—
- 3 days mental cleansing;
- 3 days of mental rest.

Schedule for the 7-day mental cleanse—
- 7 days of mental cleansing;
- 14 days of mental rest.

Schedule for the 21-day mental fast—
- 21 days of mental cleansing;
- 1 month of mental rest.

Hint: If you fall off the wagon, it's alright. Simply skip one day and start over again. If you complete the 21-day mental cleanse, then you have created a new habit. During your cleanse, limit your exposure to the news, newspapers, or negative people.

Caution: Do not take this exercise lightly. It is challenging and will take a lot out of you, but you will also learn a lot about your thought patterns and yourself. You will witness many subtle, yet incredible results. It might be trying at first, but don't worry; this is a normal part of the distillation phase. Negative thought patterns will diminish through the heat of either your conscious focus, or your outer circumstances. Make sure the positive prevails.

Caution: Do not share this exercise with anyone until you have completed one of the three sets successfully.

Use the 3, the 7, or the 21-day schedule whenever you feel the need to eliminate a buildup of "mental waste." This will balance you. Make a note of all of the significant things you experience, feel, and think of during your cleanse since this could be what you are attempting to force out and discard.

The Power of Conscious Choice

How many of us believe that we choose our financial crises as a way of learning? How many of us believe we choose the moods and the states we want to be in? We do, in fact, choose whether we want to be stressed out over money, feel hopeless or helpless in its grip, and we choose whether we want it to cast a long, dark shadow over all of the wonderful aspects of our lives. It's as simple as saying, "I choose to accept these bills; I will not worry about my paycheque being too small." We need to realize that before we got into this funk, there was a fork in the road of our minds; here we had the opportunity to choose either love, accepting our creation, or to worry about it. We need to get to a point where we're consciously choosing acceptance over fear, forgiveness over anger, and compassion and kindness over frustration. We can't always control our financial situations, but we can accept, and we can manage until we get better. The following exercise will teach you how to become more aware of your choices.

Exercise:

Name ten difficult financial situations you were faced with in the past month? What were your choices? How did you choose to face them? For the next seven days jot down the choices you make about your money. This could be the choice to pay one bill over another, or the choice to fix the roof over taking a holiday. Just be aware of the financial decisions you make on a daily basis.

Love Your Money

Consciously choosing to incorporate new beliefs and practices will dissolve your old, painful relationship with money, and it will draw to you, from within or without, the power you need to create a new financial reality. You will be able to separate yourself from your troubled financial past. Dissolution and separation are important parts of alchemy. The alchemist must learn which heavy substances need to be removed, and the alchemist must also combine new substances that will mingle together harmoniously. Your increasing self-awareness will give you power.

The quality of the relationship we have with ourselves is what makes for powerful money choices. If we torture ourselves, our ability to make wise money choices will be diluted by a negative power, and we won't make much progress. You have to redefine your relationship with money so that you learn to love your money. How can your money choices be any good if you hate those choices, distrust them, or fear them? Most people are afraid of money. Many lack a basic understanding of it, and what we do not understand, we generally fear. Many who have money are so afraid of losing it, afraid of how they might be shunned, labelled, or judged without it, that they cling to it for dear life. Others are so afraid of money that they repel it before it has a chance to enter their lives. In these misguided relationships, money is anything but neutral. Ultimately, you determine when money will enter and exit you life. The next exercise will help you to redesign your relationship with money.

Exercise:

Find a stack of bills and some paper money. First touch your bills, then your money.

1. How do you feel about your bills? Do you realize that the bills were created as a result of the choices you

made in the past? What would you like to change about the bills you receive in the future? Are you proud of your bills?

2. How do you feel when you touch your money? Are you fearful about losing any of it? What impressions or images arise as you touch it? Do you trust yourself with it? What would it feel like to have more than enough for all of your wants and needs? Are you proud of how you got it?

3. How do you feel about your overall financial-health? Are you headed in the right direction? Resist the urge to define your choices as good or bad. Look instead at how your choices have been affecting your overall financial health.

Make a point of finding out where your beliefs and choices about money originate. Can they be traced back to friends, parents, siblings, or relatives? Start digging. Even though these beliefs may have been unconsciously learned, recognize that you did choose them. Now it is time to commit to consciously choosing your own financial states and responses.

The Power of the Word

When we were born we saw light and we heard sound. That light is still within and around us. It is everywhere, nourishing us. Most of us communicate with the world through voice, by talking. Our words have the power to create and they influence. Think about some of the things that we say: "Eat!... You're fired!... You're hired…. Now!... I love you…. I hate you….We're broke….You've won!" All of these words are rife with energy and they have impact. Do we give any thought to how they might be received, not only by another person, but also by our own subconscious filter—a subconscious that stores and hoards everything like a pack rat?

I am still living with the consequences of my own words. Five years ago, after my divorce, I went back to Italy to visit my best friend and my ex-husband's family. What I didn't realize was that I was still carrying a great deal of sadness and anger. I hadn't recovered from my divorce and I missed the people who used to be such a big part of my life. On my way home, I took the train to the airport. The conductor asked me for my ticket. It was a return ticket so he asked when I would be travelling back. I told him, "I'm never coming back here." Those words were said with such intense emotion that it has been almost seven years since I last saw those people. Every time I try to plan a return trip, something comes up and the trip is delayed. I willed a destiny with my words, and only love and compassion can undo this. Now I must work very hard to clear up that imprint. We have to choose our words wisely because what we think and say will shape our futures. Our words have the power to evoke, detain, enforce, entrap, hurt, destroy, calm, soothe and heal. The funny thing about words is that they never come alone; they bring their friends with them—feelings. Words can inspire all kinds of reactions in the mind and body, further reinforcing our future word choices, thereby digging a deeper hole for our financial future to fall into, or building a sound platform for it to rise upon.

I have always believed that when we use profanity it's because we lack, in that moment, the very words that describe how we're feeling. So why not incorporate new words? Why not expand your vocabulary by adding new words? Make a point of learning one new financial term each week and incorporate these words, at least once, into your speech. New financial words can come from your bank statement, your tax form, your RRSP or 401K statement, mortgage papers, or loan documents. List them all, then either call up the office for an explanation of the term, or go hunting for the definition on the Internet. Once you've exhausted that list, get a book on financial planning, or accounting for beginners. (I list some that I've relied upon in the past on my Web site.) Every word you come across and you don't understand, jot it down and then research its meaning. Learning more about financial jargon is empowering, and with every new word, you will feel your power increasing.

The Power of the Question

Of the seven stages of alchemy the "Stage of Questioning" can be likened to fermentation. When we ask ourselves questions, the mind instantly searches for the answer. If it cannot find it within its own sphere of influence, then it will search for the answer externally. The process of fermentation involves incubation and gestation. Sometimes we feel like we are stagnant, but in reality, this is a period of incubation; during this period, the mind is still at work, searching for an answer, searching for a way for you to reach your goal. Think about the hourglass on your computer screen that keeps turning, telling you to wait while it searches for your request. Why are you reading this book? Why are you experiencing financial pain? We've got to constantly ask questions, and mostly, we have to question ourselves.

Children are always asking questions and nine times out of ten they get their answers. I remember how I used to ask myself many more questions when I was younger: "I wonder what he'd say if I called?" Nowadays, because I'm sooo smart, I've got a gazillion answers and only a few hundred questions. Yeah right. Ask the bank if they would consider giving you that loan. If they turn you down, ask why? Ask if they could offer you any suggestions on how to get a loan in the near future. Ask the owner of the house you want to purchase if they'd be interested in holding a second mortgage. Ask yourself what it would feel like to have more than enough money for all your wants and desires.

Exercise:

Name five things you truly want to have your money do for you. For example, I want to—

1. Start a university that bridges the money divide;
2. Have an investment portfolio of $25,000 by…;
3. Become an influential writer;
4. Achieve financial whealth;
5. Save $10,000 by…

Now list them as questions to yourself, for example—

1. I wonder how I could start a financial university that focuses on bridging the monetary divide between people?
2. How can I create an investment portfolio of $25,000 by…?
3. What do I need to do to become an influential writer?
4. How can I achieve financial whealth?
5. Could I save $10,000 by…?

Ask yourself more questions. Make new choices. Invest in new thoughts and respect your words. Fill yourself up with things that make you happy. We draw energy from things that make us happy when we really need it and you will need it as you make your changes and move towards whealth.

Do you know why you have a bank account? Do you know why you have credit-card debt? Why do you even have a credit card? Come with me and we'll follow Alice down the rabbit hole. Using the question, "Why do you have a credit card?" as a springboard, let's see what we can dig up.

Q: Why do you have a credit card?
A: Because I need one.

Q: Why do you need on?
A: To restore my credit rating quickly.
Q: Are there any other ways to restore your credit rating quickly?
A: I don't know.
Q: Since you've gotten the card, do you know if and how the card has improved your credit rating?
A: No, I don't know.
Q: Then how do you know if it's an effective way to improve your credit rating?
A: I don't know.
Q: How can you find out?
A: By requesting my credit report from the Credit Bureau tomorrow.

Try it, I guarantee you'll find there's a lot you don't know, but you can learn how to improve your financial health. Here are a few more... With some investments reaping 30%, why is your bank only paying you 0.5% on your savings? What is the credit-card fee based on? Why does the bank charge us for using our own money? I was questioned once about something very trivial that I assumed I knew. The question was "Why do you clean your home?" I blew off the question and said, that's easy, I want it to be clean if company comes over. Not satisfied with my answers, he continued asking me... eight more times! Here were my seven answers. I clean—

- when people come over;
- because where you live should be clean;
- so people don't think I'm dirty;
- so I don't have too much mess piling up;
- because no one else will do it;
- because I have to;
- just because! (I wanted him to leave me alone, already.) It seems that my friend wanted me to think about pos-

sibilities, making me realize that there can be several answers to any one question. Often, when we look for an answer, we are looking for something specific. By doing so, we exclude other potential possibilities. After my friend drilled me with questions, I finally discovered the real reason why I clean my home—because it gives me clarity. This was revolutionary!

Financial alchemy guides us through our internal explorations and it teaches us to actualize our revelations. Financial alchemy is about unifying, polarizing (or focusing) and re-harmonizing all of our life energies. In short, it is a state of financial grace.

Chapter Eight
Financial Grace

The art of graceful living requires a sense of balance. When being financially enslaved becomes too painful, you will begin to make financial-wellness a priority. You will aspire towards whealth because it will be your opportunity for freedom.

Building a solid foundation in money management is not the easiest thing to do. You will have to be patient, diligent, and committed. You will have to have faith. Building solid whealth from the inside-out will be one of the most physically, mentally, and spiritually challenging exercises you will ever face. Financial grace does not mean that you will always balance your budget or that you'll never make another ridiculously expensive purchase; financial grace allows you to accept your challenges, and it means that you will always search for and find a positive solution. It implies the need to recognize and utilize the tools always at your disposal, tools that will balance your finances before a crisis erupts. Financial grace requires that you choose to remain grounded in chosen financial values and principles, especially in uncertain times.

There are five elements to financial grace: Values, Options, Time, Trust, and Balance. When combined, these elements increase your financial stability and they take your "bottom line" to a new level.

Values

When choices, which rule our course of action, are rooted in values they become our life foundation. Our values are our shield against a pace of life that is running at break-neck speed without a fixed destination. And so we try to keep up. It's the keeping up that begins to lose steam. When our values are clear, we are guiding the train. So what are values? Why are they important for your financial-health? How do you even begin to build a financial life around them? These are all valid questions, but we need to start at the beginning. A value is the soul of your choice. It is what moves it, and what gives it direction. Values ensure that the choices we make are meaningful. A value is what's left after you strip your wants clean and lay them bare; they are naked, and you cannot run from them. You may not be ready to accept certain values at a certain time but they are who you are, what you care about most, and they lay at your centre. Your values may be showing you where you're selling yourself short. Values also change at different times in your life, so it's a good idea to reassess them during particularly significant points in your life.

With this in mind we begin the process of finding our values. On a sheet of blank paper, draw a line down the centre so that you have two halves. On the top left, write "Wants," and on the top right, write "Values" (Quality or Essence). Start with your wants. List everything you've ever wanted, not received, and aspire towards, no matter how trivial it might seem to you. Following is a chart to help you get started.

Wants	Values (Quality or Essence)
Purchase a house	**Tradition**: reunions with myself and family
Ability to continually afford monthly trips to the hairdresser and aesthetician	**Financial:** consistency
Travel	**Cultural experience**
Take courses	**Knowledge**
Fresh flowers in home daily	**Beauty**
Buy organic foods regularly	**Health**

The last thing to do is to highlight three words or phrases in the "Values" column that best describe what is at your core. You should try to be as succinct as possible so you can get rid of all the extraneous stuff and cut to the chase. A list of values might look like this—

- living near trees,
- being with good friends,
- travelling,
- interacting with people of different cultures,
- dancing,
- listening to music,
- taking courses,
- reading,
- wearing good quality clothes,
- being competent in business, like I could hold my own,
- writing instruments and paper,
- computer knowledge,
- teaching my daughter strong principals, and how to love herself,
- being home to help with homework,

- healthy hair,
- luminous skin,
- quiet time for myself,
- speaking and learning different languages,
- keeping a strong connection to my Source,
- balance,
- harmony,
- stimulating conversation.

Now you've identified your values, the things that drive your choices. You'll want to decide if you want to keep a particular value, or not. Does it really reflect who you are, or who you were? One example is "valuing other's opinions." Since it's the opinion that is the central value, one way to modify this value is to focus on "valuing your own opinion." These values are important to your financial-health because this is where you will derive your meaning as you begin to restructure your financial life: your budget, purchases, savings, and investments. If you don't start by incorporating values, making a budget becomes a bunch of numbers that have little meaning. Think about it—we have all been there before—we let our emotions rule in the heat of the "purchasing moment," and we end up sacrificing our values because we have purchased outside of our values. At the end of the day the necessities still need to be bought. Values make the numbers personal. For example, if you discover that one of your values is beauty, then you would include a category for beauty in your budget. By doing so, you've actually allocated funding for something that's important to you. Even if you budget $20 for beauty—it could be a face cream, or a bunch of flowers (a simple bouquet bought once a week)—you have responsibly devoted a portion of your budget to an important value. How you decide to spend the allotted amount is entirely up to you. This is one way your values will direct and support your financial-health. Other ways will be mentioned throughout the book.

Options

An option is having more than one choice, and options don't limit you to one simple outcome. We feel terrible when we have to remain in a job that we have long outgrown, or that has become suffocating to remain in—simply because we "can't afford to quit." If I had a penny for every time I heard, "I can't afford it," I'd be rich. When you are financially healthy, you have the option to leave a job you have long outgrown, feel morally compromised by, or are undervalued in—just as being physically healthy allows you the freedom to bound up a flight of stairs without the aid of an inhaler or an oxygen tank.

The whealthy have options and options create opportunities. When you are financially healthy, you can do things like purchase a home with a rental unit in it, and this way, in the eventuality of a financial crisis your mortgage payments would still be covered by the rental income. By taking out a RESP you give your children the option of attending university. If your child's focus shifts and he or she decides to become an artist, these savings could put a roof over their heads while they "find themselves." By investing in IPOs (Initial Public Offerings), you create an opportunity not only to purchase stocks in a company you can scrutinize closely before it gets listed on the stock market, but also to buy them at bargain-basement prices and sell them higher (if you've done your homework).

With so many choices available today, it becomes an increasing challenge to know what we really want, to decide what we don't want, and to honour what we do have. Having options is having abundance. When we choose our options wisely, we bring value and purpose to our lives. The whealthy have a surplus and this surplus provides them with the option to invest, either by allocating the surplus in real estate, stocks, RRSPs, RESPs, 401Ks, high-yield-offshore-investments, new businesses, or in education, either for themselves or their offspring—all of which will experience a future increase in value. When you choose an impoverished, or a just-above-broke consciousness you are in effect choosing to have limited options. You are choosing to have only one place to send your kids to for learning; to have a house with a mortgage and only one way to pay for it—your paycheque; to pay more in taxes than any other group of people; to pay more for products as inflation rises without seeing any dividends. The name of the game is growth, and if what you shell out doesn't grow, you're just treading water, barely surviving. As teens grow up, life under their parent's roof seems hemmed in— limited by restrictions the parents have established. As they mature, they envision various options: college, marriage, career paths—all of these seem possible to a teen. However, they feel restricted by the walls of their home and one day they wrestle the courage to say, "This is what I want. It's mine for the taking. I want to try this." Our money is alive with a life of its own: it is an exuberant teenager waiting to grow into an adult, and we need to give it options and opportunities. It's dying to get out there and "perform" for you, to grow for you, but you limit it to things that kill its spirit, you don't give it a chance to do things for you. How can it grow when you send it down one singular path and tell it to "walk this way" only? In this way it cannot create, it cannot play, and it cannot grow. Our money needs options to grow, and it needs many outlets so it can bring back a bounty far greater than the little worm we dangled on the end of a hook. We all know that if we are not growing, generating more love, more compassion, more whealth, then we are surely in a state of degeneration.

Time

The whealthy take the time to plan and look ahead. They don't scramble at the last minute if they've been fired, scrounging up money so they can survive until they've landed the next job. They have emergency funds and they plan for trips months in advance so they can get the lowest possible price. They don't break the bank to pay for an unexpected, emergency flight. Believe it or not, the whealthy rarely pay retail for anything. They've taken the time to research how to obtain the best quality item for the lowest price. The whealthy take the time to plan and they have patience. People who are near broke are generally impatient because they haven't taken the time to plan or prepare. Often times, the near broke person doesn't even know which bill is the most urgent, or where they can buy the cheapest groceries. How much time do you dedicate to budgeting and becoming familiar with your bills and expenses? How much time do you spend speaking with creditors when working out a financial crisis? Do you ask your bank manager if they could offer you a better mortgage deal? When did you last take the time to educate yourself about money?

Realize that righting your financial wrongs will take time. You have to honour this time and have patience during the process—eventually, a whealthier you will be revealed. You will want to push things along. You'll think things like, "If I pay $1,500 for the best credit repair guy out there I'll be back on track in no time." You'll want to jump to conclusions because you can't stand the wait: "This isn't working for me. My family has always been in financial crisis. It's just who we are." I'll warn you, it won't help matters if you rush things along, or if you make negative predictions. Real results take time. I can assure you of this. Resist the urge to compare yourself to those people who are further along the path to whealth. Comparing yourself to others is like plucking a seedling from its pot to see if any roots have sprouted; you will only destroy the progress you have made. Recognize that you are feeling impatient and continue your journey. Choose the path to financial-health, no matter how often you err or doubt.

Give yourself the gift of time—time to sit and plan

ahead, time to set financial goals and monitor your progress. Take the time to financially educate both you and your kids. The rich view time as a commodity. The poor believe that money is the only commodity, and that's why they are always trying to gather more money—while the rich try to gain more time. Give yourself the gift of taking a long-term perspective on your financial life. Instead of looking only three weeks down the road, start gazing at three months down the road, and then three years. What do you see? What do you want to see? This is not a race and you are not competing with anyone but yourself. You will not be judged by the financial planning gods. Take your time. I'm sure you've heard this before. We are all unique individuals who have different needs and wants. Financial stability can be gained if you learn to move at your own speed. I'll tell you again, "Take *your* time. No one else's but yours." Yes, our society is one that thinks, talks, and inter-acts in nanoseconds, but you can slow this process down by taking *your* time. I went through three years of financial frustration and depression because, at the time, I chose to invest my money in my new business. Much later, I grudg-ingly understood that this was not the healthiest choice for me and I went back to work. Ten months later I was laid off. Things were financially tight, for a very long while, and I bitterly struggled with my choices, and the financial posi-tion they had placed me in.

During that long period, the one thing I had was a lot of time. I struggled with this because I didn't want time. I wanted money! Eventually, I came to appreciate the gift I was given and I saw how whealthy I was because I had time. In the nine months following my layoff I started my first book. I took courses that rerouted my career. Time allowed me to take a breath, find my footing, and ground myself for the first time in my adult life. I strengthened my sense of self-worth and recognized an opportunity: I had to carefully envision the kind of employer I wanted to give my time to the next time around

There are two types of satisfaction: material and non-material. Material satisfaction occurs when you purchase something like a video; nonmaterial satisfaction is the act of sitting and enjoying the video, alone or with someone you love, whether it's your kids, your lover, or your friends. Financial satisfaction results when you learn to balance the material with the non-material, and this balancing act requires your attention and your time. Give yourself the gift of time; it is the second ingredient of financial grace.

Trust

I remember my financial turning point. I knew I had hit the bottom of my trust reservoir when my husband questioned me about a dollar I had asked to borrow from him. (I needed it for groceries.) When he had asked me what I needed the dollar for I was both shocked and humiliated. Now, my husband was not unkind or miserly, rather, his reaction was based on my past financial history. We eventually divorced but remained good friends, and it cannot be denied that our individual relationships with money were a major cause of the marriage's demise. He did not trust me with money, and this hindered the journey I so badly needed to take in order to find whealth. Now, as I reconstruct my wallet and my pool of trust, I want to enter my next relationship without any financial baggage. I don't want to be deficient in money or trust.

What is trust? I can sure tell you what it isn't, and we all know when it isn't present in our relationships. But do we know what it is when it is present in our lives? We intrinsically link trust with expectation. I mean, if you expect someone to do something and they come through, you trust them. If they don't come through, you don't trust them. Really though, repetitive behaviour builds expectations and not necessarily trust. Expectation focuses on *eventuality*, or the end result of what you want to happen. Trust invests in people and allows for any outcome, putting stock in what you will learn and how you can grow. Trust is allowing the outer experiences to change you; it's creating and maintaining many openings simultaneously; it is letting go and knowing you are safe and that all is right no matter what others tell you. Expectation, on the other hand, is the acceptance of a certain view or set of values between two people, or with yourself. Expectation creates and maintains only one opening because it is about hanging on, hoping things will work out in the preset way you've come to rely upon. Both approaches can be used in the achievement of financial-health; however, expectation involves an element of fear, and trust does not. One carries with it unspoken pressure, and the other does not. Neither is essentially good or bad, but you must decide which works best for you and when to use one over the other.

In Money We Trust

Ever wonder why some banks are called Trusts? Even though most of our trust in these organizations has eroded, the currency that international business revolves around still says, "In God We Trust." Money has become almost synonymous with trust, yet how much of this is really true when it comes to our own individual money issues? If something happens in our lives and we are unable to pay our debts, we are suddenly branded untrustworthy. Nowadays, businesses don't trust you unless you put down a deposit, provide a co-signer, or if you present a VISA card (preferably Gold or Platinum). People are signing prenuptials as a declaration of trust. In certain situations these practices are needed, but I do want to emphasize that whenever we choose to interact in this manner, we give up something else that is harder to regain than a lost dollar. We give up trust. Any financially responsible individual who makes a withdrawal from their bank account will, at their earliest opportunity, replace it with an equal or greater amount. Are we sure that many of the things being substituted for trust are of equal or greater value? We trust that if we get a raise we will be better off financially; if our sons and daughters become doctors and lawyers and make good money, we trust they will be well, whole, and complete. We trust brokers that get us big returns. If we win a million dollars today we trust that our lives will miraculously right themselves. Employers trust that their employee's desire for money will keep them showing up every day at 8:30 and leaving at 6:30, later even—if they want that bonus. For the majority of the working world it does work, but more and more companies are experiencing record-high turnover rates, sick days, and absenteeism within their organizations.

We trust all of the above when it comes to money, but how many of us trust that we can change our own financial lives? Do you trust yourself with your own money? Do you trust yourself with $1,000 in your favourite store? Do you *trust* that you have what it takes to make things better when faced with overwhelming financial circumstances? Do you trust that you have what it takes to maintain financial-health? I'll bet you had a particular idea of what you wanted your finances to be when you had "enough." Right? That is my point—expectation is not the equivalent of trust.

The erosion of trust isn't just happening within our financial world, it's happening on a much more significant level…it's taking place within ourselves. Think about how little trust you have in yourself when it comes to money. Be honest. Did you say you would pay a bill when you knew darn well that you couldn't? Did you say you were broke when in fact you had a $50 tucked in your wallet, just so the other person could pick up the tab? Did you use your money to buy other people gifts so you would be accepted or loved, not trusting that you already were? In order to improve your financial-health, it is important to begin with small steps, and one of these steps should be rebuilding your relationship with money, ensuring that trust is a central element. This exercise will help you cultivate a greater degree of trust.

Exercise:

Dedicate one day, preferably a Saturday or Sunday, when you don't have much on your "to do" list. On this day continually ask, "What should I do now?" and then go and do whatever thing your deeper self suggests you do. After you have completed one action, ask again, "What should I do now?" It might be sitting in silence for 5 minutes, or for 50 minutes. It might suggest that you simply watch your breathing, or you might be directed to pick up a certain book, go to a particular place, or call someone.

Note: This exercise lets you trust that you do know what is best for you; that there is a wisdom that guides you and provides for you and that you are safe to let yourself be a part of it.

Balance

When you begin to emerge from financial crisis you feel wobbly at first, and you're uncertain if the purchases you make are the right ones, or if you should even spend a dime at all. The thing to understand about balance is that it's not always about perfection—sometimes you miss the mark. Balance is about the overall well-being of your financial affairs. If your financial well-being is on one side of the scale, what is on the other? Is it other people's perceptions, an unrealistic lifestyle, or the picture-perfect family that lives in your head? Or is it things you value, a holistic view of your life, or a Greater Purpose you're ready to commit to? To get a sense of the balance that needs to be achieved, draw a see-saw, just like the one in the diagram. Put your financial well-being one side, and on the other side, put those things you currently care about. Now ask yourself,

Did any of these things contribute to my financial crisis?

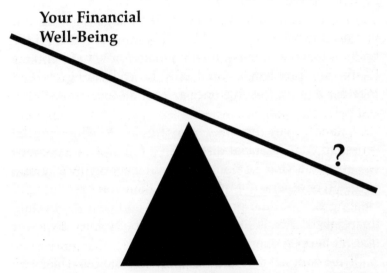

**Your Financial
Well-Being**

?

Now, don't panic. You can change—if you are willing to invest some of your time and energy. Your financial balance will be restored and supported by financial education, commitment, trust, and time. A balance is an apparatus for measuring weight. It has a central pivot and near the top there are two arms with receptacles that move higher, lower, or remain even when objects are placed in them. When you can sustain financial-health, you are balanced, neither higher or lower than you should be; you are not so easily swayed or moved by intricate marketing campaigns, slick ads, savvy salespeople, or worse, by yourself. When you reach a point of financial balance your desires become aligned with you values: the essential qualities you want your life to be based on. You're more aware of what you want, or don't want and you're beginning to honour what you have—and if you live anywhere in North America, you probably realize that you have more than many of the people in this world. What you have worked on in the previous chapters is what is known in accounting circles as "trimming the fat," or getting rid of the excess. You've started by trimming the inner surplus to make yourself more receptive, or financially lean and trim. We are taught that money is an adhesive that holds things together, but you need to ask yourself, *what* is it holding together? If it's holding together a mess, then no matter how hard you try to fix the "problem," you'll only be continuing to hold together a mess. Resolve once and for all to achieve financial balance.

Balance takes time. You're not going to eliminate the causes of your financial distress in a few months, perhaps not even in a year, so don't waste vital energy by blaming yourself, or others, if it takes longer than you first thought. Healing is a gradual process, so grin and bear it; building financial balance is like getting your body into shape—it doesn't happen overnight.

Trust yourself to make wise financial choices. This book is your guide. Some of the exercises might resonate with you more than others, and you will have to trust your own intuition, thereby focusing on the methods that bring you greater results. (But don't decide that something doesn't work before you try it. It won't always be easy.) You must do the mixing. You must be the alchemist of your own financial grace. I believe in you.

Chapter Nine

Living Below Your Means

The phrase "living below your means" has many negative connotations. If you're living below your means, people often assume that you are in financial trouble. When you are living below your means, some people might conclude that you are in denial of your wants, that you've been downsized, laid-off, or worse, that you actually *need* a budget because you're not making enough of an income, which really means that you're not valuable enough to be earning a steady income. All these assumptions! In general, it's believed that living below your means is a circumstance forced upon you—seriously, who in their right mind would *choose* to live below their means? Yet, living below your means is essential to building whealth. Simply put, it means that in order to have the seed with which to grow your money tree, you must *keep* more than you spend. In this chapter we'll look at the new mentality you will need to adopt in order to save more of your money. We are going to take apart the pieces of what it means to live below *your* means, and then put it all together again so that this practice becomes clear.

Living below your means is like living beside a strange family that you've never met. (You've heard all kinds of fascinating stories about these unusual neighbours, but you've never actually shared a conversation with them.) Really, you don't know these people at all, but you feel like you do, and to be honest, your not sure if you'd ever like to meet them. Finally, you meet them, and no doubt about it, they are odd; however, in some ways, they are also the most pleasant people you've ever met, refreshing beyond belief because they are so unusual. The same goes for living below your means—this is a daunting concept that you will grapple with because you've imagined so many negative possibilities, and you've drawn all sorts of erroneous conclusions about this lifestyle. What you'll find, however, is that when you finally start to implement this practice, it will be as if someone has opened all of your doors and windows, letting the fresh spring air into your gloomy, confined space.

What does the idea of living below your means mean to you? Do you think it means material starvation, or that you'll be labelled a freak because you're different? How about that you're incompetent or maybe you're poor? It's time to uncover, and dispel, the negative perceptions you have in regards to "living on less." That's right, open a door within your mind and throw away all of your misconceptions! Great, now we can start on a new page. Keep on your guard though, they'll be back to bang on your mental door, wailing about how you can't make it. Talk to them through that door, but don't ever let them back in—you've got work to do. This is the part that may involve change, not the shave your head and move to Iceland kind of change, but real change that entails conviction and trust. True whealth does not tolerate escapism.

Lifestyles: Living for the Moment, Paying for Years

Most of us end up in debt because we try to support a lifestyle that we can't really afford. This lavish way of life is addictive, and it becomes like a drug that we cannot live without. Many of us feel compelled to work longer hours so we can make more money to support our habits; like a junkie searching for a fix, we always want more. It's a false high. Where exactly did our natural state of being go? How did we get to be here? Is the lifestyle we've chosen even our own? How many of us can say that our lifestyle really supports who we are? How do we turn this behemoth around? As you will discover, I am not speaking so much of change as I am of the discovery of a more congruent pattern of life—a congruency aligned with your values. An authentic lifestyle, as we know, cannot be bought, try as we may; it must be discovered, carved, adapted, and crafted from the artist's hands—your hands.

In order to find your own genuine lifestyle, you must first pay attention to your way of life, or daily existence. (Sounds familiar right? We covered this in Chapter Six.) While searching for your lifestyle, I recommend that you begin by requesting a receipt for every purchase you make, and then you should record your purchases in a booklet as soon as you get home. This kind of rigorous accounting will help you in several ways. For one, you will become aware of your spending habits. I suggest that you review your "purchases log" at the end of each week. You might find yourself asking, "Did I really need to buy that tacky cat figurine—just because it was on sale?" The next time you are tempted to make an impulse purchase, you might think twice! Keeping your receipts will also make returning items much easier. If you do this exercise for 30 days, you will learn a great deal about your spending habits. While doing this exercise, one of my retired clients discovered that most of his money was being spent on food. (His wife was already buying their groceries.) Another client of mine realized that she never spent any money on herself. Admittedly, she did put some away in her savings, but because she had never treated herself, she felt cheated. My daughter, who is 11, was reimbursed seven dollars after going over her receipts because she discovered that the cashier had made an error. She had saved her receipt and when we recorded the information, we noticed that there had been a mistake. Once you get in the habit of tracking your purchases, you will be released from the confines of habitual, senseless spending—eventually.

In the late 1980s the American designer Donna Karan made a fortune from a line of clothing she called "Seven Easy Pieces." This wardrobe consisted of seven essential clothing articles that a woman could either dress up, or down, simply by pairing them with the right accessory pieces. The "Seven Easy Pieces" were not flashy, exciting, or provocative, but they were definitely functional, versatile, comfortable and sleek—American sportswear at its best. We too can pare down our lifestyles so that they are sleek, practical, and versatile—without forfeiting beauty.

A Return to Values

Let's return to values. We don't need to fix upon a particular number but you will begin to notice there are between five and seven essential values on your list that motivate you, not only in your lifestyle but in your purchasing-style too. Go back to your core essentials list and select the values that are most important to you at this time in your life. If you come up with six or eight, that's okay: we're not splitting hairs. Your core essentials will become the cornerstone of your lifestyle, your purchasing-style and your budgeting-style from here on. List your seven future core values and make sure they are the ones that matter the most.

1. _____

2. _____

3. _____

4. _____

5. _____

6. _____

7. _____

Budgeting-Style

Now, get out a piece of paper and create an oblong box across the page. Divide this box into the number of core values you arrived at earlier. Gather all of the receipts that you've dutifully gathered from the previous month and slot each one into a corresponding category. Next, simply make a check mark for every time you've spent money in support of any of your core values. For example, if you have a receipt from Starbucks, try to find a corresponding value that it represents, and make a check in the box. You might find that this purchase does not match any of your values. (You're tempted to mark the value box labelled "health," but are you being truthful?) If, on the other hand, one of your receipts is payment for a monthly gym membership, then tick off health because it does indeed support this value. If you have a receipt from IKEA, tick inside the "home" column. At the end of this exercise what you will have is a very realistic picture of your current lifestyle. You might also find that you are rethinking some of your spending habits. Next, create another sheet, only this time use different headings (these may or may not be your values). Some examples might be entertainment, dining out, grooming, or clothes. Do the same thing that you did previously for all other receipts you have not ticked off and list each under a value. Scour the page and be honest. Any column that has several check marks denotes one of your core values. Include it in your list of values, or if you have a column that does not have many (or any) check marks, remove this from your list. Remember, your values will change as you become more and more financially aware. Take another look at where the majority of check marks fall. Are there any signs of imbalance? Is there one column that outweighs all others? For example, when I did this exercise, I was astonished to find that 26 of my 73 transactions were made on food. *Food!* I also realized that only *one* of my transactions involved savings. The other column that surprised me was my "home" column. Why? Well, I rent! I was spending a lot of money on a place that I was going to be moving out of eventually! I'm not saying these purchases were useless and shouldn't have been made, but when I looked at my core values list I realized that none of my major money transactions supported a sense of accomplishment, generosity, openness, or expansion. These were my values at the time. If I had been supporting my desire for openness, I would have spent more on travel, but "travel" was nowhere among my columns. Or, if I were supporting my need for accomplishment, I would have put more towards marketing my business. I realized that my everyday transactions did not consciously include my core values. Looking at this table will definitely give you an indication of whether your lifestyle is in balance or not; whether you're supporting your life's core values or not. If I had done this exercise before I went bankrupt, I would have seen that my spending habits were not aligned with my core values. I could not afford the way I was living and I had lost touch with the values that supported my dreams and goals. I was lost. My head had been buried for too long and when I finally looked at the landscape I had created, it was too late—my bubbly energy was gone and I felt totally incapable of digging myself out of the financial mess I had gotten into. Bankruptcy seemed to be my only alternative. If only I had known how to verbalize the word "no," my financial demise might have been avoided. What you'll learn is that saying "no" to yourself, setting limits, is an essential tool that will allow you to conjure whealth.

"No"—An Essential Financial-Health Food Group

Change is inevitable. We are powerful creatures, but we cannot control all of our circumstances. This frightens us. (You mean the world does *not* revolve around me? Whose cruel joke is this?) As we get to know ourselves better, we come closer to a state of whealth. Getting to know yourself is a very frightening process, and sometimes this fear unsettles you; it looms ahead like a shadow and instead of going within and shining the light, you turn your back in avoidance. Often, we avoid being alone by padding ourselves with more: more clothing, a bigger home, a fancier car. Really, by grasping for happiness in these "outside" sources, we are refusing to acknowledge the voids of our inner selves. We tell ourselves we deserve to feel good (even if it is borrowed) because we've worked hard for life's little luxuries—we deserve that $300 dress, little care is given to whether we can afford it or not. North Americans are going into debt because we don't know how to tell ourselves that one simple word: "no." Why is saying "no" wrong? Why do so many of us carry huge credit-card debts? Why can't we just say, "No, I cannot afford this right now?" "No" doesn't have to mean "never." It can mean, "No, not right now," "No, not on my card," "No, not at this price," or "No, not in this store."

Any way you slice it, it all boils down to self-discipline. I know, I know, when you think of self-discipline your mind is conjuring up nightmares of military academies, harsh parents, and a life of deprivation. But if we can't tell ourselves "no" when it comes to spending, eventually we are leaving the door open for someone else to do it for us. Think about it, do you really want a credit-card company telling you "no"? It seems that while many of us want freedom, we still want someone to tell us what to do. When credit-card companies extend us credit and we abuse it, we are allowing them to take on a parental role. The truth is, we don't want to take full responsibility for our financial-health. We want a part of that responsibility but not all of it. We want a cold drink of lemonade on a sweltering summer afternoon, but we don't want to prepare it or wash the glass when we're through. When we are ready to claim our financial freedom, we must be willing to claim it all: every senseless purchase, every loan, every money goal missed or accomplished, and even every gift or item bought unnecessarily. When we accept responsibility, we claim a power that will give us confidence and allow us to heal.

Abuse of Trust

Recovering from abuse is a tough journey. Anyone who crosses the finish line is victorious. In this race, it doesn't matter where you place, finishing the race is what matters. Great, fine, but why are we even talking about abuse when this book is about our relationship with money? You need to recognize that credit-card debt is about abuse; bankruptcy is about abuse; living *above* your means is about abuse. An abuse of trust. Whose trust are you abusing? Your own, your kids', your family's, and the institution that you made the initial agreement with, that's whose. Your family trusts that you will keep a roof over their heads. Your spouse trusts you to spend $100 on groceries, not just $75, while the other $25 goes towards a sweater. When you signed the papers to finance that flatscreen TV, you entered an agreement of trust with a company. When you became old enough to sign your name to the back of a credit card, you trusted yourself to make wise money decisions that would advance, not deplete your financial-health. If you don't believe the notion that unreconciled debt signifies a breach of trust, just look at the name of the people that are in charge of your money if you decide to file for bankruptcy: *trustees* in bankruptcy. Trust me, it's no coincidence they're called this.

Abusive relationships are about control and power. One party is too trusting and the other party has manipulated this trust, twisting it to serve its own selfish needs. In most cases, both parties are weak, either physically, emotionally, mentally, or spiritually. They feel some degree of powerlessness. When you have $100 worth of cash or credit, you have the power to buy anything, anything you want within that price range. This is an enticing sense of power, especially if you are floundering in other areas of your life. When you purchase something with that $100 and it does not support your core values, you have committed a breach of trust. When we are in financial crisis, the circumstances are very similar to those of abusive relationships, but they are not so obvious. In response to these trying circumstances, we begin to spend and expend because we desire control. We spend because we feel weak and power*less* and then we lose trust in that divine place within ourselves.

When you begin the journey towards financial-health, you are actually agreeing to restore the trust you once abused and lost. This restoration is gradual and occurs over time. If you find it hard to come to terms with this fact—that change is gradual—there is a greater chance that you will repeat your old mistakes a few short months, or even years from now. Repeating old mistakes is a product of foolishness, not destiny.

When the whealthy leave behind money for their heirs they make sure the money cannot be accessed before a certain age. (Usually the heir will receive their inheritance when they are in their late twenties or early thirties.) By setting up these kinds of restrictions the "elder" can ensure that the younger heir is mature enough to be trusted with the inheritance. I suggest we start building our own funds of trust: pools or reservoirs that we can dip into and that are filled with trust first, and money later. You can begin by walking around with $50 in your wallet for one month; during this time you will be conscious of the money, but you won't spend a cent. When you have achieved this, bump the time to three months, and then increase the dollar amount to $100. Do this until you fully trust yourself, and the world around you, to carry $1,000 in your wallet without using it, or being afraid to lose it. I guarantee this little act will incrementally increase the trust you have in yourself and others. Gradually, you will fill your pool of trust.

Living below your means is a combination of four

things—recognizing and fashioning a lifestyle based on your core values; making sure that any purchase, no matter how small, supports your core values; using the simple word "no" more often, especially before making a purchase; and understanding, then healing your abusive relationship with money by restoring your trust fund. Once you've tackled these monsters, budgeting and monitoring your money will simply become a natural consequence of your combined efforts, not an effort in itself—as natural as the placenta leaving the mother's womb after a birth.

Chapter Ten

Financial Goal Setting

Let's liken financial-wellness to physical health. Many people care about their health and in order to encourage their physical well-being, they routinely engage in physical exercise, they eat right, and seek professional-medical advice when the need arises. Some people even take preventative measures, such as using natural remedies to prevent the possibility of illness. Losing weight has long been the number one New Year's resolution in the United States. It's like being in an accident: you aren't hurt, but when the medics arrive, your pulse is racing, your blood pressure is sky-high, and you're not making much sense when they ask you questions. You might think you're okay, well enough to drive home or resume your day, but you are wrong. Financial-health is a lot like physical health in that most people don't have a clue if their pulse is beating too slowly or too rapidly for the financial transactions they're engaged in, and most people don't even know if they're financially coherent or not. Many people don't have a good grasp of their level of financial-health, or they are too afraid to deal with it until it's too late.

When our bodies are free of dis-ease every part pulls its own weight. If one area of the body is sick, this means that other parts of the body have to work a bit harder in order to compensate for the weak link. Imagine if more than one malady was afflicting your body all at the same time! You would have barely enough energy to get through the day. The same disaster happens to our financial-health when we abuse our money. We become so financially out of sync that sickness easily takes hold. To illustrate this point, let's imagine that money is our blood; our blood pressure is our net worth; our heart rate is our cash flow; and oxygen is our passive income. Buying a house and taking on a mortgage isn't a bad thing; it's just a shot of adrenaline that makes your pulse beat faster. The body adapts to the quickening of the blood flow, but the heart, liver, and kidneys do have to work a little harder. (Nothing to worry about though, because you're in good shape, still young, and your body will recover in a short time.) As time passes, you decide that you want to renovate—first one room and then another and another. You borrow the money from the equity in your home. Christmas arrives and you don't want to look bad (what kind of scrooge are you if you can't even give at Christmas?), so you buy nice, not even expensive, but unbudgeted gifts. Everyone's happy. Here and there you've bought yourself some clothes—always when they're on sale—and good grief, it's summer now and the kids will be expecting a vacation. Our blood pressure and heart rate are now above normal, but we don't really notice the trouble we're getting into. How could you know? Isn't this situation normal? By now we are heavily relying on credit cards, we're barely making ends meet, then oops, a parent gets sick and can no longer take care of themselves. Not going to happen to you? Is everyone in your home relatively healthy? Okay, oops, you get laid off, or your spouse does, or your kid hits someone with the car and you get taken to the cleaners in a lawsuit, or you suffer from burnout and have to quit your job. Any number of these things can happen in the game of life. Now you're hyperventilating (the body's attempt to bring more oxygen in at a faster rate), and trying to grab at money straws to fill the holes because your blood isn't clotting—and it won't clot because it's too thin. The fact is, you've spread yourself too thin. Instead of creating more passive income over the years (it would have given you more oxygen, allowing you to "breathe" easier), you were short-sighted and thought only of the moment.

Since we have likened blood to money, consider this fact—there are 5 million red blood cells, 10 thousand white blood cells, and 250 thousand platelets in a drop of blood that is the size of a pinhead. So if you'd like to convince yourself that you just don't have enough resources to get out of debt, read the previous sentence again and think of the abundance that the body continuously creates. There is nothing that proves we don't have the resources to improve our financial-health.

Checking the Vital Signs

Our heart rate can indicate poor circulation and in the case of financial-wellness, our heart rate is like our cash flow. Cash flow is the amount of money that flows in and out of your life on a regular basis. How well does your money circulate? Does it come into your hands, only to vanish in the nearest shop, or does it get as far as your RRSP or 401K plan? When a part of the body doesn't receive adequate blood circulation, it decays. In extreme cases the result is gangrene, the area affected must be cut off so it doesn't affect other areas. If one of your financial "bodies" doesn't receive adequate funding it will become diseased and it will begin to infect other areas of your life. This is why creating a passive income is very important. If your main source of income, such as your job, becomes irregular or is discontinued, you'll need some kind of back-up plan. If the body loses blood, it needs to be replenished, and the same applies to your financial well-being. When you've lost money you need to repair this loss by increasing its flow and monitoring its consistency. We can't expect that our jobs will always be there, so we need to take measures to continually improve our cash flow. We have to ensure that we will always have a consistent supply of "oxygen," no matter what happens. One way you can increase your cash flow is by purchasing a carefully researched rental property with your current home equity. You can also increase your cash flow, and your job security, by attending school in order to upgrade your credentials.

Net Worth

The next vital sign we must monitor is our net worth (assets minus liabilities). A negative net worth could kill—plain and simple, just as surely as high or low blood pressure could. So what is the "ideal" net worth? Doctors say the optimal blood pressure rate is 120 over 80. For optimum financial-health the ideal net worth should always be (knowledge + action) over money—more knowledge than money. Right now you're probably scratching your head wondering if I'm crazy. I am not saying that you should choose knowledge over money, but I am saying that at any given time you should have more knowledge than money. Still don't believe me? Ask yourself this: "Why is it that many self-made millionaires claim that if they lost all of their millions today they could make it back in a matter of a couple of years based on their knowledge and their ideas?" That's because their knowledge is *greater* than the sum of their financial assets.

Getting Clear

Gaining clarity when it comes to money is a challenge for most people. Clarity doesn't mean that you will instantly know all like an oracle. Clear thinking means that you *know* what you want, why you want it, and that it "fits" you, your lifestyle, and your values. At this point, the "how will I get it?" part of the equation is irrelevant. How does a light bulb work? I don't know and I don't really care. I just want it to work when I flick the switch. Are you with me?

When I refer to clarity, I am speaking of the clarity between you and your Source, be that God, your inner self, or your inner voice. I am not speaking about clarity between you and the financial goal you wish to attain. (This will come later, once you've found your Source, or Greater Purpose.) The Source—your centre, or core—is that part of you that knows the truth. The space between you and your Source needs to be clear; everything else is random and cannot be relied upon. Find out if your goals resonate with this place. Consult with it and always make sure it is clear of worry, stress, fear, and anger. Even when life is hectic and full of distractions, it is imperative that this passage remain clear. A lack of clarity is one of the greatest afflictions of our society. In a society where there is so much choice and so much opportunity, how do we decide what is truly best for ourselves? If you aren't clear about what you want and why you want it, it's easy to get trapped into purchasing things you don't really need; trapped into a place where financing the purchase lasts longer than the object itself.

When seeking financial wholeness what exactly do you need to get clear about? Here are a few starters—

1. What is my goal?
2. Why do I want this particular goal?
3. When do I want to accomplish this goal by?
4. How will I know that it's been accomplished?
5. How will I feel when I've accomplished it?
6. How much time will I need to accomplish it?
7. How much will it cost me in the end? (After taxes, financing fees, and depreciation.)
8. Is it worth it?
9. Does it support my core values?
10. How truthful am I about my commitment to achieving this goal?
11. What is the life expectancy of the item?

Do I really want financial-wellness and do I feel deserving of financial-wellness? Oddly enough, these should be the two most important questions that people coming out of financial crisis should ask themselves, but rarely do.

No amount of help in the world can heal someone if they want to die or feel they haven't the right to live. A very good friend of mine was dating a man who suffered from a very low opinion of himself. He was an extremely talented actor and screenwriter, but he couldn't even find the money for groceries. While they were dating he was also seeing someone else who he believed he was in love with, but this woman treated him like he was meaningless and showed him no affection. My friend was aware of this, but she cared about him deeply and so continued to date him. She thought the situation would teach her about unconditional love. She spent many nights telling him how gifted he was, that he needed to love himself more, and that he had to recognize that what he felt for this other woman wasn't love, but masochism. During one of these talks he got angry and asked, "Has it ever occurred to you that I might *like* my situation just the way it is?" She realized that, no, it had never crossed her mind! How could someone actually like being treated this way? For that matter, how could anyone *like* being in financial crisis, in debt, or bankrupt? Well, the truth is, no one *likes* being broke—once. Just like no one likes to break a bone once. However, if you suffer from a rare disease and your bones always break, you learn to live with this until a cure is found. Likewise, people learn to live with being chronically broke, or making ends meet, or living on borrowed money. The good news is that being chronically broke, or just above broke, is not a rare disease and it can be treated. You can be financially healthy again. Good financial health does not begin with saving your first $1,000; rather, it begins with saying "yes" to financial wellness, recognizing that you *deserve* to be financially healthy no matter what financial follies you may have committed in the past. This reality must resound throughout your whole being—you've got to want it more than the habit. Do I really want financial-wellness? Do I feel deserving of financial-wellness? If you can't answer "yes" to these two questions, you won't be whealthy, no matter how much money you make. If the answer is no and you're not aware of it, then the incongruence between the answer and any effort you put towards recovery will be a dismal waste. Get clear on this before you move on, even if it takes a while. Clarity is an essential part of recovery.

Setting Financial Goals

Okay, so now that you've gained greater clarity it's time to start looking into the future and deciding what it is that you want your money to do for you. This is when you begin setting your money in motion. It is at this point that money starts working more for you and you begin working less for it. Setting goals is about gazing at all the quantum possibilities that lie ahead of you and saying, "This is what I choose to focus on; this is what I desire to have in my life." By setting your goals you are becoming the architect of your financial future.

Look again at your list of values and create two financial goals for each value. Remember, attention is the currency of the new economy and not all of your goals are worthy of attention. Be realistic about your goals. Challenge each goal to the 11 questions, and put them to the test. If you judge the goal to be worthy, fine, but any goal that doesn't make the grade should either be trashed or relegated to a "more consideration required" pile. Some values could be—education, savings, retirement, investment, car, home, entertainment, giving, clothes, travel, personal, kids, or business.

Now zoom in on each goal and decide whether it is a short-term goal (6 to 24 months) or a long-term goal (2 to 5 years), and then choose a target date by which to have each one accomplished. Some goals will be completely achievable and others only partly, but you still want to acknowledge and give yourself credit for achieving even a portion of the goal. You'll know if you've accomplished the entire goal because you'll recognize it in its wholeness, but how will you recognize if you've achieved a partial goal? Here's how—for each goal there are the bleachers, first, second and third base. If your wildest dreams for any given goal came true, what would they be? They're the bleachers. First base is the essential quality of that goal, second base is the minimum you want to achieve, and third base is the entire goal when accomplished.

This is a specific example—

Goal: To purchase an income property on my own credit.

The bleachers: To purchase a duplex with less than $5,000, with the owner agreeing to extend a second mortgage from the equity he or she has in it.

First base: A sense of financial advancement.

Second base: To purchase with a co-signer, a single family dwelling worth $80,000 - $125,000.

Third base: To purchase an income property on my own credit.

What you're doing is creating a framework for your money. The achievement of your goal now has parameters. Whenever you acquire extra money, support one of the goals you've identified.

Creating Your Budget

From time to time, issues will arise out of the blue and they will need your attention, your money, or both. I'm talking about situations like the death of a close friend or family member, getting married, getting divorced, having kids, dealing with a family member's addiction, a lawsuit, taking care of an aging parent, or taking care of someone who is terminally ill. If this happens, will you have a money pool to draw from? Do you have adequate insurance coverage? These are all important questions to consider when creating your budget.

When you're creating your budget, it's important to recognize that life happens and certain things can't be budgeted for—that's just the way it is. Setting financial goals allows you to build a framework for your money. When you budget, you create a vessel for whealth so that when money comes to you, either through your paycheque, inheritance, tax return, or by any other means, it has somewhere to go. The rich have portfolios, stocks, and real estate to hold their money. These vessels take them to a place of whealth.

Step One: Since we always begin with paying ourselves decide (*now*) how much you want to put in the savings category: $25, $50, $100, $500 a month (you can always adjust it later). Whatever the amount, try to save 20% of your income. So, based on a $2,500/month income, that would be $500/month.

Step Two: List all of your expenses and then list all and any income over the last 30 days (if you did the exercise with the receipts you've saved yourself some time). Subtract your total income from your total expenses, the remainder is your *immediate* cash flow. Do this once per month.

Step Three: Now decide what lifestyle changes need to be made; what can stay and what needs to be exchanged or given up altogether? You might ask yourself some tough questions like—could I take on a tenant? Could I move in with my parent(s)? Could I trade in my car for a more economical one? Can my kids pitch in to help pay for some of their after-school sports or their back-to-school clothes? Make sure that the important categories are taken care of, that you have money for yourself, even if it's $5, and get a buy-in from every single member of your family—meaning everyone is in agreement and you're all working toward the same thing.

Step Four: Increase your income. This could be through the purchase of real estate, selling your skills or expertise outside of your job, licensing your information, landing a second job, or looking for a higher rate of return on any money invested or saved.

Step Five: Chart it either on an Excel spreadsheet or on plain, old graph paper and stick to it. Stick it on the fridge, or stick it on your door. The main thing is that you *stick to it*.

Step Six: Appreciate every single penny that comes into your possession, from 5 cents to a $5,000 bonus. Appreciate money in all its forms and you will be amazed to see how your money appreciates for you. In many ways money is like a puppy. It is only waiting for a sign of appreciation from you, its master, to perform and do things for you.

You have created a personal or household budget, you've calculated your net worth, and you know your cash flow. Does it end here? No, it doesn't—especially if you've just suffered any sort of financial crisis like bankruptcy. If you've ever been sick, you know you need to see the doctor more often than when you're in good health. Well, when you're coming out of a financial crisis, you need to check your financial health against your budget. It's a good idea to check your budget once per month, your net worth once per year, and your cash flow every three to six months. Why do I suggest checking them so frequently in the beginning? This is because actively monitoring your progress lets you ensure that your actions are dictated by your goals, not your habits.

Chapter Eleven

Staying Your Course

The Naked Millionaire isn't simply a book, it's a course too. *The Naked Millionaire* is a course for the course of your life. Most of us like to hear that our lives are on course; it makes us feel good, like we haven't been wasting our time, that we aren't complete losers, because, hey, we're heading somewhere. When we think of staying on course we picture a straight line from A to B, never veering for the slightest moment. In reality, life is more like a golf course than it is the path of an arrow. Even if you've never played golf, you've at least seen the pros face their own challenges: getting that little, white ball from its starting point to the last hole. In as few strokes as possible they must navigate ponds, sand pits, inclines, and curves in order to win. Their course is anything but a straight line leading from A to B.

So how do you stay the course to financial-wholeness without giving up or giving in? First, find out which combination of the course—including core elements—fits you and your circumstances best (we will approach each element of the program in more detail in the following chapter). Getting that right combination is much like golfing; there are a few basic strokes that everyone uses, but each player uses them in their own ways. The game of golf is personalized.

This course is structured in the same way, in that I show you the elements and you personalize them. It's important to make a commitment to your course for 12 months— that's right, one full year. Give yourself this time. There's no question, many things nowadays can be done in a short space of time, some even immediately. However, whealth cannot be instantly achieved. What must be instant, however, is that you take action. I will discuss this in greater detail a little later.

On our course to financial-wellness we too need to situate ourselves in a supportive environment, and this includes inviting supportive people into your life. At this point, it's probably a good idea to discuss supportive people and supportive environments. Supportive environments are all the elements of your life that contribute to the positive reinforcements of your dreams and goals. This could be your desktop wallpaper, music you love that lifts your spirit, paintings on your walls that transport you closer to your core, the thoughts you entertain and the words you use, for example. Supportive people are part of our supportive environment. They cheer us on, point out roadblocks or simply share similar experiences so we don't feel so alone on the journey. They can be friends, family, your personal coach, or a mentor. Imagine a situation: you've fallen off the wagon and purchased a set of dishes you really don't need—but they were on sale and you couldn't turn down a great bargain. In this case, you could choose to understand that you're still recovering. You're still weak and so you could take the dishes back, or you could decide to keep them and take the money out of next month's budget. You could berate yourself with verbal abuse: "I knew I couldn't stay on track, and now I just wasted all that money on those stupid dishes." At this point, you could lose all of your resolve, saying, "Good grief, and I've got another 11 months of torture left...I just love that new sweater that so and so bought, and it was only $10 bucks! I'll just buy the sweater this week and start the program next week." The choice is yours: you can support or harass yourself—you decide.

Sports pros schedule regular appointments for their practice sessions. We need to do the same—set up an appointment with yourself, with a coach or someone supportive, be it every Friday, Saturday, or Sunday. On this day you're going to do your budget for the next week, monitor and compare how you've progressed, and decide how you'd like to act differently with your money in the next week. (Don't forget to applaud your accomplishments.)

During the week (any day other than your appointment), only deal immediately with those money matters that are pressing or urgent—everything else gets scheduled for your financial-health appointment. There is one other thing that could take you off course—sometimes permanently—and it's fear. The antidote lies in the following pages and it can be tailored to any individual situation.

Vitamin A(ction) - One-A-Day

When I was writing this book, I came to realize and accept that I had to do whatever it took to support my craft until it was strong enough to support me. What this meant for me was that I had to get a job that would provide me with an adequate income. As I was going through the motions of looking for a job, I became fearful of not finding one in time. After some reflection, I realized that my fear would ease (in an equal degree) if I took one action toward supporting what I said I would do. I did three things that very same day—I called a publisher, I took on a newspaper delivery route, and I wrote—and my fear went away. Do at least one thing today, and everyday, that propels you toward your goals. In this way, you are supporting the course of your life and dispelling your fears. Remember, *whealth = knowledge + (action over money)*. Do you doubt the power of one action per day? One action per day is 365 actions per year. Each action brings you closer to your goal. For me it meant e-mailing my network of contacts to ask for job leads, writing the marketing plan for my book, making calls to the corporate world for freelance writing work, and following up with e-mails and calls. Each and every day I had to commit to doing at least one thing that supported my financial goals. Now you're probably thinking that you can do more, and you probably will complete more than one action a day (any action over one is a bonus that increases momentum.) The thing is not to stop, don't miss a day without taking your Vitamin A. If you are tempted to engage in a whirlwind of action to convince yourself that you're making progress, to speed up the process, or because you simply don't believe a lot can be accomplished with a little, try to relax. In the case of financial recovery, more is rarely better. Whatever your action for that day is, be it making the bill payments, calling for quotes, enrolling in a class, purchasing a newspaper, and reading the business and financials too, do just that one thing. You may have a list of things to do for that day, but the key is to identify the one thing you know that will push you forward, toward your goals. What you'll find is that taking initiative—acting—will give you control over your future whealth.

Compounding

Compound interest is one of the most powerful money tools we have at our disposal and yet it is not fully understood by most. It is incremental in nature and really begins to develop after about three years. This same system is at work in your daily-supportive action too. It also is incremental and builds on itself, until one day—*boom*—you're out of the gates at lightning speed wondering how you've accumulated so much money, so fast, with so little effort. This is how daily-supportive actions work. You see the years pass quickly whether you run yourself ragged or whether you take your time, so get off the treadmill. No one's chasing you.

The United States of Awareness

Going through a financial crisis causes us to be more

aware of our weaknesses and strengths. We are made vulnerable. Financial dis-ease makes us aware of the time that we have allowed to slip through our fingers and of the time we have left. In some ways, a financial crisis provides us with the opportunity to truly discover whealth. When we experience financial trauma, our whole Being shifts, and we can either grow or wilt.

A shift in your state of Being is simply a shift in landscape and scenery within yourself—your world. The United States of America is a complete body of 50 states. Some states are more popular to live in than others, but nonetheless, they are unified. Some states are more prone to hurricanes, high crime rates, and nasty snowstorms, while others enjoy low crime rates and gorgeous weather 75% of the time. Despite these variations, they are still the *United* States of America, not the "Some-Are-Great-While-Others-Aren't States of America." As you travel the course of your life you may experience various states: the state of bankruptcy (financial or otherwise), the state of marriage, the state of depression, the state of ecstasy or euphoria, the state of grief, the state of poor health, the state of whealth, or the state of peace. As you travel the course towards financial-health you will pass through many states: the state of depression or sadness, the state of abundance, the state of joy, the state of knowing, the state of appreciation, the state of anger and frustration, the state of anxiety, the state of wanting, or the state of fulfillment. All are united within you, and you may travel in and out of these states a few times every day or week, but you will only take up residence in the state you want. A pro golfer doesn't choose to play in a state of fear and panic, but, in the course of a championship game, if those feelings do arise, he or she will ride them out until a more positive state returns. A state of panic might erupt when you settle down to do the mental fast or budget. You might feel lethargic when it's time to go to the bank, reach in your wallet to put the $20 into your savings account, or you might feel confusion when you approach your One-A-Day action requirement. The worst thing you can do is ignore the feelings you have; they are valid and when you face them they seem less frightening. Acknowledge your state of Being and gently move on to what you know is right. Follow your core values and be assured that you are progressing.

I too know what it is like to be afraid and frustrated. When I first started on my financial-wellness course and made a budget, I visited the state of anger many, many times. I hated doing it even though I knew it was good for me. Then I went through the state of lethargy and would put it off for as long as I could. Now that I've gotten into the habit, each time I keep my money date I exist in a state of calm and relaxation because I know I've completed that basic element. You might find some activities easier than others. I've always liked collecting my receipts, because tracing my expenditures made me feel like I was practicing awareness and that I was in control. So you see, during the course you will visit many states of being, and this is okay. Just choose the most positive state you can enter and approach each task from there. One quick and simple technique is to envision your preferred states as rooms in a big house. Decorate each room by taste and energy level. So when you choose to enter a task from a state of joy, simply enter your home and go into the designated room for joy. Stay there a moment, see yourself doing the task in that room as you absorb the quality of joy. When you come out, do your task and notice the difference in your level of energy.

Whenever you are dealing with your money, whether physically handling it, speaking or thinking of it, try to direct yourself out of any of the negative states and approach your finances from one of the more positive states of awareness. If you've ever travelled through an urban area that you know to be crime-ridden and poverty-stricken, you don't think to yourself: "Hey this looks like a great place to find a hotel room for the night!" What you want to do is get out of there as quickly as possible. No one wants to live in a rundown, high-risk community. So why would you want to live in a negative state of Being in regards to your finances? Again, I'll say, when money comes to you in *any* amount—baby bonus cheque, tax refund cheque, paycheque, birthday gift, gift certificate, child support payment—treat it with respect, hear yourself speak of it with appreciation, and think of it with love and not with fear or worry.

Starting Money Traditions

A tradition is a time-honoured practice, or a set of practices, passed on from one generation to the next. The rich set up trust funds as a tradition, they hand down heirlooms, pass on their financial knowledge to their offspring, and many make their children work for whatever money they earn. These are some of the traditions that our "make-hay-while-the-sun-shines" society has lost or forgotten. Think of how much you could save if your mother left you the three carat diamond ring her mother gave to her. If you are enjoying a family heirloom now, then someone created a tradition of saving—a money tradition—to make this a reality today. This is part of our problem. We can't see past our noses and we're so busy toiling for today that we forget about tomorrow. (We certainly aren't thinking about our children's tomorrow.) We need to leave something for the future—not only a reservoir of money, but also a deep sense of appreciation, gratitude, and joyful promise. We need to teach our children financial grace. Professional athletes like Michael Jordan, Tiger Woods, Wayne Gretzky, and Muhammad Ali, all of them are role models that have left us with a tradition to follow, a tradition of excellence and fortitude. Each one of us is a role model for our children. We show our children what they are worth, what they should expect. We have a whealth of knowledge that we can give to our kids, so let's make sure it's positive, that it supports their greatness, and inspires them to achieve more, not less. My daughter, who does the course with me, visits her father in Italy twice a year. She recently returned after the Christmas holiday and proudly reported that she had remembered to ask for her receipt while buying ice cream. I couldn't have been more proud. I realized that I had passed on a tradition of appreciation and the value of money to my daughter! It was powerful. It was positive. I was changing the course of our lives through very simple lessons. No, I don't yet have a pile of money to pass on to my daughter, but I will one day. I'm proud because the practice of obtaining a receipt after every money transaction is one money tradition that I've passed along. Here is a very short list of some money traditions you can start. It's a good idea to expand this list by adding some of your own ideas:

- using cash more than debit or credit cards for small purchases,
- practicing making purchases based on your values,
- paying bills no later than one week after receipt,
- paying the lowest price possible for things you use every day, such as phone rates, groceries, travel, dry-cleaning, gas, etc.,
- celebrating Christmas on December 25th , but exchanging gifts in January to take advantage of sales,
- keeping good records.

Starting a money tradition means getting the whole family involved. It means taking the time, allowing time for actions to compound, and honouring your commitments to financial-health.

The Vortex

The other day I was meeting with some peers. We all volunteer for a non-profit organization that helps turn kids into entrepreneurs. We all have different careers. After being laid-off for almost 10 months, I came to the decision that my next career move should support my writing, and hone my skills as a writer—I chose to get into freelance copywriting. As a single mother I chose this over an immediate, steady job because it afforded me the time to be with my daughter *and* finish my book. Finally, I thought, I am making wise choices that will drive me forward, not backwards, sideways, or around in circles. I was new to the writing field and I still hadn't secured my first client, so naturally I still had doubts. By meeting with this powerful group of individuals, I noticed something else that happens when we commit to a particular path: the energy of the people and things around you creates a vortex, and draws you towards them. Let me explain: as I sat there listening to them speak about their work, all good paying and exciting jobs, I started thinking, shucks, maybe it's better if I *do* get a steady job. I felt I was being drawn in by some magical spell, pulled closer into accepting their reality as something that "should" be mine also. This was not their fault, nor were they conscious of having this effect on me. So what was happening?! I was being drawn in by the energy of their shared beliefs. These people shared similar values and thought along the same lines: A nine to five job is secure; a title is a sign of success; improving your skills and working for a big firm is the clearest, shortest path to financial fulfillment.

None of these beliefs were wrong—they just weren't mine. They did not encompass my values. That night, as I briskly walked back to my car, the cold January wind whipping, I shook myself loose of the vortex that was slowly drawing me in. I discovered that my endeavours were, and are, just as valuable and important to me as my friends'; I chose to follow my own path and I devised my own expectations.

This same phenomenon happens when you commit to

something like financial-health. All kinds of forces will try to draw you into their world, asking you to accept certain beliefs and denounce your own. For example, well-crafted advertisements depicting decadent lifestyles can influence you, making you believe that happiness can be found in a product. Don't underestimate the power of their tactics. It can seem as though you're under a magical spell: "three easy payments of $49.99—no applicants are turned down, (and here's the killer)—even if you've been bankrupt!" Sometimes, when you are in the company of friends who are talking about their latest purchase, a great vacation that's costing a bundle, or the big-ticket birthday gift they're giving their kid, you can feel the pressure, the tug, the pull. Here are a few things that will keep you out of the vortex and on course:

1. Recognize that everything is energy, plain and simple. It's not the heavens conspiring against you that keep you feeling a certain way, and it's not bad juju either—just energy in motion.

2. Be still. The fastest way to get dragged under if you're ever stuck in quicksand is to struggle and fight. But remaining still slows the process, keeping you alive that much longer so help can come. So when you're feeling frantic, slow your breathing down and try to still the movement around you and your thoughts.

3. Remember your values—this is who you are, you can't lie about this one. In my case I value writing more than a title, a corner office, or a fixed salary. I know where I stand.

4. Keep your money meeting. Repetition counts and this process will eventually act as your own internal Instant Messenger if you ever veer away from your goals.

5. One-A-Day supportive actions have a tremendous impact on building up your resistance to the attraction of the vortex. Doing your One-A-Day supportive action

feeds who you are, leaving you feeling satisfied, not constantly hungry for external gratification, or validation. In the beginning it may not seem like much, but like compound interest, it reaches a point of critical mass where it starts to work on its own. Then you will find the courage to say no, and the conviction to purchase in line with your values.

Escaping the vortex is like experiencing a near-death experience. You've survived; you're more grateful and direction is clear. This heightened awareness allows you to monitor your progress and make adjustments throughout your course to financial-wellness.

Monitor Progress, Make Adjustments, and Keep Records

How will you know if you're off track? You don't want to wait until you're overdrawn and the bill collector or bank manager calls you. Someone has to keep score—and in this game that means you. How else will you know if you're winning or losing? The referee or the umpire might be the most hated person on the field, but he has the final word. You can rant, you can rage, and you can shout all the expletives you want, but he's only calling 'em like he sees 'em. You'll probably hate and curse them in the beginning, but your budget and your list of One-A-Day supportive actions are the officials on your route to financial-wellness, and they have the last word. These directive tools are neutral and devoid of opinion. Let's take a look at how these tools help you monitor your progress and make necessary adjustments.

When you begin your One-A-Day list of supportive actions you should write an entry for each day. Over a period of as little as a week, this sheet will give you a good overview of the potholes in your commitment—or where you've been true to your word. Days without an entry—even if you've done the act, but failed to write it down—

means you're not yet willing to support yourself. The purpose of writing down your actions is so you can keep track and monitor your own progress. You will be able to review each week and feel confident that you completed seven actions that supported your financial-health. Then, once a week, when you get together with yourself for your financial date you will assess your financial progress and your shifting attitude towards money. One of your entries might be—

- remained positive about money all day (Don't scoff, this is no small feat when you're digging yourself out of a money hole),
- researched potential streams of income that I can pursue,
- set goals for the year,
- called to set appointment to have credit counselling,
- set up automatic withdrawal from my paycheque to a new savings account for a slush fund.

If you're like me, you might have three or four items on your list that you'd like to accomplish for the day. This is fine, but it's important that you identify one very important task. If nothing else was achieved that day, finishing this one task would give you a sense of accomplishment and forward movement. This is critical when applying the One-A-Day principle to your course.

In the game of baseball, following through a swing is key. When watching the game you might think that it's the power of the initial hit that propels the ball into the air. However, upon closer inspection you'll see that it's the follow through of the swing that really completes the motion. Think about it—the player is crouched, his eyes are on the ball, and he focuses on where he wants the ball to land. The ball is pitched, the batter swings, hits the ball, continues with the swing, and then he runs. If he doesn't follow through with the swing, then it's a mere bunt and we know how far those go. Got the idea? The same reasoning can be applied to our approach to finances. We stare down our fears, focus on where we want our efforts to land, and we make a commitment to put $25 into our savings by tomorrow and we follow through by doing it. Tomorrow comes and—what was that? You forgot, you got held up, or your kids got sick? If you don't follow through, it's a bunt and this won't get you very far, will it? Following your decisions through is essential. Follow through keeps you moving forward, and once you are moving, it's easier to follow one action with another. If it's your habit to fudge your follow through, don't be surprised if you find yourself bunting your way through this course. So what if you do miss a shot, for whatever reason, and you don't quite make the financial markers you've set for yourself? Like any pro, you have to practice and keep practicing. Your money meetings are your practice sessions and over time you'll find out what actions (mental or physical) bring you the best results. On days when you miss, or hit the ball out of bounds, get into a better position and try a different hit. Remember it's not a race; take *your* time.

This is how you keep track, monitor progress, and make adjustments on your course. The budget in the beginning will reveal areas that still need improvement (feedback). Your One-A-Day list shows you how your interest or energies are being compounded (feedback). Some days, you will be very proud of your progress, and other days, you will notice that you have faltered. I suggest you take the good with the bad, don't beat yourself up, and keep going.

Waiting—Three Days of Grace

You will be tempted. There's always something out there that you feel you've just got to have. While you're on the course to financial-health, if you really feel compelled to make a purchase, give yourself three days of grace. Wait three days and think it over and here's the trick—leave yourself open to the possibility of receiving this item in many different ways. You might stumble across an item of even greater personal value, and it might come to you easily. Let me share a story with you: a very good friend of mine intensely desired a red chair for her home. One day, as she was leaving to run an errand for her baby, my friend noticed some movers disposing of a red velour chair. It was in perfect condition. The owner was helping the movers and my friend commented on what a nice chair it was. The woman asked her if she wanted it because she was about to set it outside for Goodwill anyway. She accepted the offer and received what she had been wanting—and for free! Take my advice and give yourself a three-day grace period. If an item comes off the market before you are able to have it, it wasn't meant to be.

The Truth About Motivation

For as long as I have lived, I've always heard that in order to accomplish you goals you've got to be "on" and motivated. If you aren't always feeling "on", well then, there must be something wrong with you. This is incorrect. The most important thing I've learned about motivation is something I learned from reading *The Right to Write* by Julia Cameron. Cameron says that "Being in the mood to write, like being in the mood to make love, is a luxury that isn't necessary in a long-term relationship." I believe wholeheartedly that this applies to just about any area in our lives where "being motivated" is a suggested prerequisite. The truth of the matter is that motivation is a luxury even when it comes to personal betterment. Motivation has been fed to us as the panacea of our own laziness. Motivation is not something you do or get into, it's something you are and it happens or is triggered when you're "guided" by your values and your Greater Purpose. There will be days when you are totally pumped, and have complete confidence that you can and will achieve whealth. There will be days, many of them, when you just aren't motivated and you just don't have faith. You may struggle during the process of recovery, and you may feel that it would just be easier to fall back to your old ways (hey, it's not like you were living on the streets before, right?!). In moments like these you might feel like motivation has abandoned you, and maybe there's something wrong with you because you're not continually glowing with energy about your new commitment. Let me be honest with you right now, you won't always be motivated. Get over it. There will be days when the only answer is to simply say "to hell with motivation!" and move on. It's a luxury, I repeat, a luxury to be motivated to do the things we need to do in order to become the great beings we are meant to be. Motivation might get you going in the beginning, but it's definitely not what's going to get you to the finish line. Commitment, compassion, and structure will get you to a place of financial stability and wholeness.

Chapter Twelve

The Whole Picture

To frame or not to frame? The other day I took myself to the art gallery. I wanted a day of inspiration, away from the piddley, little details of my daily life. Once there, I felt privileged and grateful to be in the same room with masterpieces created from the body, mind, and spirits of masters like Van Gogh, Tissot, Rodin, and Monet. Inside I saw many wonderful frames, and there was even a brief history of the frame. I sat for a long time reading some noted art critic's arguments for and against the purpose of the frame. I looked and looked, not realizing what was so important, and then I knew. Our budget is our financial frame. Sometimes we need to get a close-up view to see the details and at other times we need to step back to get the big picture, but our budget needs to have more elements to it than mere numbers—that would be as limiting as painting with one colour.

Now is the time to take a good look at your big picture. Recognize that by simply reading this book, you've made the journey to another way of *thinking* about your money. Congratulations! It's been necessary to acknowledge the various elements that make up your big financial picture, but ultimately it needs to be reconstructed and approached in its entirety based on how it specifically relates to your life and the new information you now possess. As I was sitting down with the software developer for *The Naked Millionaire*, all I had was a diagram of The Big Picture scrawled in pencil on lined paper. Initially, as we were working out some details, he asked me why I wanted all this information (Values List, Financial Goals, Greater Purpose, Budget, and Actions List) together on one page. What good would it serve a person looking to find and maintain financial-health? I thought for a minute so that I could explain my ideas to him with clarity. Before I began writing this book I had a vague idea of what my Greater Purpose was; when I finally figured it out, it still only resided in my head, and I thought it was far too grand to even write down. Then I thought of my values—oh yeah, I had those written down in my green notebook. My One-A-Day supportive actions list was printed on a stray piece of paper and filed between the pages of my monthly calendar, and my financial goals were written on a paper with my net worth—all written in rough. Ah yes, and my budget was in its own folder. I knew that these pieces were part of a bigger whole—my financial-wellness. I wanted it all on one page, in one place: my Values List, my One-A-Day supportive actions list, my Greater Purpose statement, my Budget, and my Financial Goals. At a glance I wanted to be able to view my Budget, weekly or monthly, current and historical, and see how my Values reflected or supported this vital piece of feedback. Likewise, I wanted to see my cumulative One-A-Day supportive actions list for any period—not to see if I was doing enough, but to see if I was doing enough of the *right things*. The more I organized these things, the more I felt in control of the course of my financial life. It was obvious to me that we aren't reminded often enough during our busy days of the things our heart truly desires. To have any sort of impact and relevance our Values list must be in close proximity to us. We need to be constantly reminded of our Greater Purpose, of what our life is all about at any given phase in our lives.

The software grew out of my need to create a new kind of money dialogue with myself. When writing my budget during one of my money meetings, I found myself thinking, "Look, I said I was going to put $50 into my savings and instead I only put in a measly $20!" However, when I looked at the left-hand side of my screen, I saw that I did put $500 on my overdraft to bring it back to $0, and hey, I finally paid my brother back that $20 he lent me a couple months ago. From looking at my Big Picture I could see that even though I didn't achieve *all* that I set out for myself, I was still *heading in the right direction* and this is what really matters.

I continued an inner dialogue with myself, and I found myself asking many imperative questions. If I changed my values, how would my budget change? If I contemplated making major purchases or multiple smaller ones, I also need to be reminded of how doing so could affect my values. Did I support myself in specific ways through my actions? Or was this cloud of action that I engaged in for the last seven days just a smokescreen to hide my fear of succeeding financially? This kind of dialogue needs to happen in our relationship with money. We can't just ask, "Do I have enough for this? Or, yes, I need this because I've worked so hard over the last few months and I deserve something special. Or, have I contributed enough to RRSPs this year?"

All of these components were not available to me in one place. No one had provided the tools to view all of these things together while still doing the necessary, and sometimes tedious, tasks of budgeting or figuring out my net worth. At the very least, while performing these tasks I wanted to be reminded of why I was doing them in the first place—and that no, it wasn't just about money. I wanted, at once, to see the big and the small pictures. It does little good to come from a doctor's appointment only to be told, "Good news, your heart is in perfect health, but your bladder, liver, and kidney could fail you at any moment." I could have gone to a financial planner and paid them to fix my budget, but other parts of my Being would remain neglected and this could only lead to another lapse in my whealth. My desire for financial-wellness was stronger than my desire for a placebo, so I kept looking. I wanted to see how it all made sense *together*, how it all fit into the grand scheme of *my* life, not just the life of my money. As humans, we have learned to see things in pieces, but essentially we crave wholeness because unity provides us with a sense of well-being.

If you choose to follow the cyber route, I've created the software and it's available for you to integrate all aspects of your financial recovery in one page—frame and all. You can find these tools at www.thenakedmillionaire.com

The Web site walks you through the steps of how to create your own money-frame page. This page can be updated daily, weekly, or monthly. You can easily view your current financial activities and compare them with your past financial history.

If, instead, you prefer the pen and paper route, that's fine too. Take a sheet of blank paper and design a page similar to the diagram shown on the Web site, using the same headings. Make 12 copies, one for each month. You will, of course, substitute all numbers and entries with your own. For example, if in the month of January your phone bill increases, ask yourself why? Were you feeling down, or in need of some support from your friends, or were you making up for not being with loved ones during the holidays? Ask, too, how this increase supports your values. Does it support your value of laughter? If it does support a value, but is still too costly, you'll want to look for alternatives when you look at your whole picture. If the increase was due to not calling or being with loved ones over the holidays, you could have spared yourself that increase by actually *being* with them, or by mailing cards or sending e-cards. If the increase was due to the need for a quick pick-me-up, then maybe a movie or sitcom could have sufficed. If it's laughter you needed, how about doing something that you're not very good at, like skating? I tried this with my daughter and it was amazing how much we laughed at my antics. The only price I paid was that I had to be willing to risk looking like an idiot for a few hours. Like I said, you've got to be willing to give some things up if you are to grow and prosper.

Chapter Thirteen
Support and Resistance

In the stock market world "support" and "resistance" are the metres of what a tracked stock will likely do in the short term. Stock prices result from a daily battle between the Bulls (buyers) and the Bears (sellers). The winner of this battle is determined by the direction the prices actually move in. Why am I babbling on about support and resistance? Because, let's face it, deals will always arise—there will always be a house that's $30,000 below current values in the neighbourhood you've always wanted; the new car in the lot that is selling at 0% financing, $0 down; or space is open on your calendar (and your credit card) for a much needed vacation. These things will always pop up and you've got to have something to fall back on, and that something includes your goals and values.

When I first started getting on my feet financially, I spied this great house. It was perfect in every way—in every way that was—but the price. Even though my agent and I tried every effort to put the deal together, the sellers wouldn't accept, and I grew more and more frustrated. One night, while falling asleep I realized, "Hey, was this one of my goals when I initially sat down to set my vision and goals to paper?" No, it wasn't! I was supposed to feel like I could breathe financially, and maintain a savings plan. Not buy a house.

In your own financial world, support and resistance are not only indicators of how we will likely perform in the near future, but also of the daily battle we fight within ourselves for financial control and mastery. For example, if the support for our financial-health slips, then the value of our investment (in ourselves) drops. That is, the amount of what we value actually drops.

The same can be said for our resistance. The point at which we "resist" financial health is the point when we actually come into contact with old thought patterns and habits that aren't very useful to us any longer, but that we cling to out of sheer comfort. If you're experiencing excessive debt and can't find financial balance, there is something you're resisting. We all resist in different ways. For instance, a friend tells you that a company is hiring and you resist by procrastinating. You find some reason, legitimate or not, for why you can't drop off your resume. Is resistance inevitable? Yes, it is when you first begin to implement change; actually you should count on it! If you don't find yourself resisting financial changes, you'll find resistance in your relationships, or in your job. Your resistance could even be spiritual. It's just the way the mind works. Your old thought patterns are afraid of venturing into new territory. That stubborn voice in your head that doesn't care about financial-health, even if you tell it that it's a better place to be. It's afraid for you and wants to protect you from what it feels is harm. The worst thing you can do at this point is avoid the resistance or pretend it doesn't exist and influence you. It will only scream louder. This is why I recommend you acknowledge your resistance and keep supporting yourself by mindfully completing your One-A-Day Action. Another reason why resistance is inevitable is that a part of you realizes that the your resistance is your current ceiling, the highest that your current mindset can take you at that moment. The part of you that is resistant realizes that the place you want to go requires effort, discomfort, and the unknown—and the mind, once it has found its groove, will want to remain lazy. For some reason, it seems that the mind is geared for efficiencies and it likes a process or set track to run on. It does not like surprises and changes in its routine, so it resists.

What we *can* do in these moments is acknowledge the resistance. If we back away and wait, breathing through the resistance, like we might in a yoga pose, we'll slowly begin to support this new mode of existence and the resistance will break. When resistance does dissolve, it is important to reinforce your decisions. When you do this, you are supporting your chosen lines of growth, and not the old lines of financial dis-ease (or your past actions). What do I mean by this? For example, you've started saving $100 a month, but during the third month you hit a resistance level and you buy something you could have done without. Now, you risk telling yourself "what's the point, there are going to be more temptations and unforeseen expenses that will continue to wipe me out". You believe that you will always be faced with hardship, but what you fail to understand is that historical trends are only *indicators* of how you will likely perform! This is the time to stay flexible and review your commitment to yourself while acknowledging the drop in support and your resistance. Review your values, keep putting away that $100, and continue to support yourself in words, actions, and thoughts for the duration of this period—until it breaks. The act of bouncing through resistance and then landing on your support is known as "channeling" in the stock market.

Channeling is the continued movement of a stock between two price or value points. Both A and B on the following page are examples of channeling movements. Channeling is not a negative trend. Traders look for specific patterns and when they notice that a stock has been in a channel for sometime they know that it will soon break, and more often than not it will break through its level of resistance and move upward. Can you break through your support and go downward? Yes, of course. It depends on you, and what you value more—your commitment to whealth or your old thought patterns and comfortable habits. It depends on what you whisper to yourself each day and what you choose to believe in. The more you support yourself and strive for what you want, the greater the odds are that you'll break the pattern of resistance. This is what the stock market is all about: it's a game of odds based on research and history. What have you told yourself in the past? How have you dealt with resistance or setbacks in the past? This is something that people who have learned to master financial-health understand—that the money choices they make today will determine their financial state of tomorrow.

Start creating your history *now*.

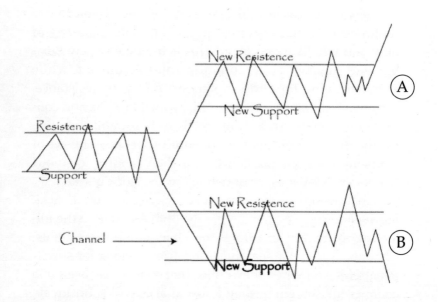

Situation

Here, resistance is caused because the person has come up against old belief patterns, they may have been in jobs that didn't nurture their pocket or soul, but they got used to it. A new job has opened up but it requires a lot of internal shifting of beliefs. They are in a channel. This could end up in one of two ways: 1) the person decides to push forward, breaking through the old barriers of outdated beliefs, into a new resistance which could look like this: they take the job, but didn't negotiate a salary based on what they're truly worth. The new resistance now becomes this uncomfortable awareness that they're not quite ready to deal with. The new support could be the new positive friends and colleagues at the new job. Or, 2) they find the leap to a new belief system too great to make at this time, or they're not positively supported to make the change so they "forget" the day of the interview or bomb the interview on the little things. Their confidence plummets, dropping through their old support level and the resistance becomes the new beliefs they were working on before they broke away from the channel.

Support

Support is the level at which you believe in the value of financial change and so you reflect this support by acting in congruence with this belief. It is the daily investment you make in your financial future. Support, as an action, can take many forms: it could be a commitment letter, following a well-planned idea, a One-a-Day Action item, or a savings plan.

Resistance

Resistance is the level at which you start to lose faith in the value of financial change. You resist progress by allowing old habits to win the daily battle. When old habits take hold of you, it becomes easier to resist, and resistance grows stronger. When you finally break free from the cycle of resistance, you will profit. For one, your new-found ope-ness will allow you to accept change readily, and as this happens, you will become an open vessel that attracts whealth.

The penetration of support and resistance levels can be triggered by fundamental changes that are above or below the investor's (your) expectations. New expectations lead to new levels of value.

The Channel

The channel is, no doubt, an uncomfortable spot to be in. But sometimes, getting to where we want to be takes being in uncomfortable spaces for a while. What's uncom-fortable? Discomfort is many things to many people. It could mean passing on the Hallmark birthday cards and buying ones from the dollar store for a year. It could mean finding new skills in the kitchen, instead of ordering take out; it could mean asking for help, or cutting off the cable for a while. It could be anything that makes you cringe, but is necessary if you are to get to where you need to be. During my first year of recovery, I stopped using a long-distance plan and I used a calling card instead. That way I knew I'd stay within budget. Once the budgeted $50 was gone, that was it, no more long chats to friends and family that lived outside of city limits.

No matter what your sacrifice is, be prepared for diver-sions, discomfort, and resistance. Return your focus to your goals and values, and if what hangs in front of you is like a vision from heaven but doesn't reflect those values, don't do it.

Concluding Chapter

Congratulations! You've come such a long way on your journey to financial-wellness. Stop now, for a moment, and relish your success. Appreciate where you are at this moment in your life, for you will never be right here again.

You've most likely chosen this book because you were facing some form of financial crisis. You've read through the book, have done the exercises, and hopefully you have a different perspective on why you ended up in a state of poor financial health. You've learned what you can do to change your relationship with money and now you can begin building true whealth based on your values. There is probably a treasure trove of information you have learned while making the journey to financial-wellness, all based on unique situations that you've faced (or are facing) and will no doubt overcome. You may have read through this book wishing you were taught these tools as a child, but remember, now you can pass these lessons on to your children. This chapter is about the importance of passing your financial knowledge along to the other people in your life. This could mean holding monthly money meetings with your kids, teaching them how to recognize their values and make purchases in line with their values. Or it could be starting a monthly money group with others facing similar challenges. In some way, shape, or form, it's important to distribute the knowledge you've gained. This will ensure that the next generation achieves whealth. Are you wondering how this can be done?

Enter the Ethical Will

A will parcels out your possessions to any heirs; and a living will outlines what you would like to have done should you ever become incapacitated. An Ethical will surpasses the temporal aspects of a life; it influences future generations with its teachings, and it is a powerful thing to leave behind.

In the past, many families were closely bound. The act of sharing and passing on values, ethics, spiritual convictions and insights about life, from one generation to the next, was greatly valued and these teaching were communicated through the spoken word. Now, because families are dispersed and scattered across cities and states, passing along knowledge and wisdom is much more of a challenge. These days, we gather to celebrate weddings, Christmas, Thanksgiving, Easter, Hanukkah, or—the reading of a will. Writing an Ethical will stipulates that you would like those who benefit from the fruits of your life to not only inherit your valuables, but also the values you have cultivated during your stay on this earth.

An Ethical will tells the story of your beliefs, your ethnic roots, important stories told to you, the values and ethics you chose to live by and why. In it you can also recount the dreams and aspirations you might have for the future generations. When you write your Ethical will, it's as if you're creating a guiding light that can help your children and grandchildren navigate their way around the sometimes murky waters of day-to-day life.

If you're reading this it means you've decided to live not only for today, but for the future. The end of your life isn't the only time to write an Ethical will. Here are some other very good times to sit down and draft one:

- newlyweds—to ensure common values,
- expectant couples—to provide a framework for child rearing,

- growing families—to ensure a common direction,
- empty nesters—to ease the transition and to formulate new aspirations,
- middle age and onward—to help translate life lessons into guides.

At any of these times, it's a great idea to sit down and tell your story.

So, What Do I Say?

An Ethical will doesn't have to be long and shouldn't sound like a sermon. You might choose to craft your Ethical will around a few chosen themes like love, loss, loneliness, freedom, anger, intimacy, or friendship. I've listed some questions below and I think they will help to get you started:

1. What is the most important thing I've learned about money?
2. What advice would I give if anyone I loved had to deal with a lack of money?
3. Do I have any advice on how to deal with a lot of money?
4. What is my definition of success?
5. What was an important crossroads and how did I deal with it?
6. What is my family history? How did they deal with money, either as a family or in couples?

Here is an example of an Ethical will:

My Dearest One:

My life has been very diverse and filled with much learning. I have often felt like Da Vinci, but since I was not living in the Renaissance, my eclectic background only served as a wedge between society of the day and the way I was guided to live. You as my daughter have wondered, many times I am sure, why I wasn't more like other mothers. The simple answer is that I could not and would not have known how to be "normal". I offer love and ask forgiveness for any pain I may have caused you in your attempt to understand and make peace with who I was and how I chose to live my life.

I leave you, I believe, with many beads of knowledge to be strung together in your own fashion and then passed on to those you love.

My definition of success is simple: the ability to manifest what you need or want at will. Be true to who you are, find and do what your heart calls you to do, and you will possess success as well as the love to manage that success. I urge you to first seek mastery over yourself, and success after, for without it you are lost.

About money I have learned this: take the time to learn about money and the principles that shape its growth. I've learned it's better to allow things to grow organically, in their own time, and this includes money. Create a good financial structure for your income to flow into and develop effective money habits as early as possible. Teach them to your children. Don't look around at what others possess; this is only a distraction that will lead you from your focus. Cast your attention, instead, to your values and beliefs. This ensures that what you apply your energies to will attract what you truly want and not just the pieces that shout the loudest.

My greatest crossroad moment came after I declared financial bankruptcy and I had to choose to learn through abundance and success, rather than lack and failure. Until then I was completely in the dark, willing to live for what seemed like a long time in the shadows of ambiguity and uncertainty. For years, while bringing you up as a single parent, I didn't know a thing for sure. I just put one foot in front of the other. Slowly, I cultivated the knowledge that the next step in my life would be shown to me and it would be the right one.

My greatest gift was in knowing love in this lifetime. I was given you to love and be loved by.

Thank you for loving me and thank you for giving me the opportunity to grow through loving you. Until we are together again, take these beads of knowledge I have gathered and make them into jewels that glow brightly for others to recognize their own greatness and be inspired by.

My love is with you always!
Mom.

Careful with Your Words

There is only one other thing to be aware of, and this is the power of your words. Make sure they are clear and that they are filled with love. Do not use this as a moment to cast recriminations or continue a feud. Those who are left with your words cannot respond or argue with you, so make sure you leave a clean slate, a bright beam of light to show the way home.

Good luck to you on your path to financial-whealth!

Index

Visit us at:

www.thenakedmillionaire.com

Learn to create new financial environments that support your dreams! Drop in today and start using the tools
that can change your financial health forever!

Here are some of the many things you can do at the site:

- Get bi-monthly, practical insights into staying your
  course when you register for the *Fiscal Fitness* e-zine.
  Learn from others' experiences; see how people just
  like you are creating whealth one day at a time.
- Take one of our provocative teleclasses from the comfort of your own home. There are classes every week to
  help you maintain your financial education at an
  affordable cost.
- Support yourself to whealth with individualized coach-
  ing sessions.
- Get budgeting software that's built around *your
  values*—not just numbers.
- Download e-books and workbooks in seconds to guide
  you on your own journey.